My Journey to Justice?

(Inside the mind of a raped man)

By

John Lennon

Shield Crest

ISBN 978-1-907629-58-7

MMXIII

Cover illustration by
Grace McLoughlin

Published by
ShieldCrest
Aylesbury, Buckinghamshire, HP22 5RR
England
www.shieldcrest.co.uk

Dedicated to my father

His Smile

Though his smile is gone forever
And his hands I cannot touch,
I still have so many memories
Of the one I loved so much.
His memory is my keepsake
With which I'll never part.
God has him in His keeping
I have him in my heart.

Contents

Acknowledgments

I have not been looking forward to writing this, and must admit that I have put it off for a long time. However, acknowledging the people who have supported me and my book is very important, so here goes.

When I first started writing and told friends and family, the reactions I received varied greatly. Why would you want to write about rape? Don't do it, John, it will set you back. Your PTSD will never get better. These were some of the more negative comments, although they were said with concern and love for me. Most people thought it was therapeutic for me and some didn't actually believe that I would write the book at all, but in general, the support I received was fantastic. To those people, and you know who you are, thank you sincerely from the bottom of my heart.

There is one very special person who deserves a very special mention. He has been in my mind, my friend, my bodyguard, my confidant, my soulmate and the one person to whom I read every word as I wrote. That person is Lee and the biggest thank you goes to him. Thank you, Lee, I love you dearly.

The Author

John Lennon was born in Drimnagh, Dublin in 1969 and has five sisters and two brothers.

After attending college in Dublin, he moved to Manchester to pursue his love of animals and worked in Manchester University Medical School for four years as a research assistant before qualifying as an animal technician and becoming a dog groomer and teacher of animal care.

He became a foster carer and eventually adopted his son, Mo. This led him to change his career, and he entered the world of social work, mainly in the area of training social care workers and working with adults with learning difficulties. After a happy and successful career in this field, he wanted to return to the animal industry and started his own dog grooming business in Prestwich. It is here that he was raped and his life would change forever.

His first interview was for *Dogs Today* magazine, which was predominantly about his dog, Indie, and her role in trying to defend him during his traumatic experience. This was followed by another for the BBC. He also took part in research for East London University, exploring the reasons why men under-report rape. He featured in a self-help guide for raped and abused men, which was produced by an editorial team comprising survivors of rape from Survivors Manchester, and published in April 2013.

He has been invited to appear on ITV's *This Morning* programme in September 2013, which will be followed by an appearance on the *Late Late Show* in Dublin.

John is currently working on his next book; "A letter To My Father?"

Preface

I started writing this book, which at that point had no title, on the way to my friend's wedding in Ireland. People ask me all the time why I wrote a book about such a dark subject. The simple answer is, I have no idea.

I suppose, looking back, I had plenty of time on my hands. Yes, I was working full time, but I wasn't engaging in normal life; dating, socialising and generally getting out and about like any other normal person. A lot of this detachment from society was because the monster was on bail in the run up to the trial, and some of it was down to fear of it happening again.

I have found writing it both therapeutic and a way of trying to make some sense of what happened to me and of people's new attitudes towards me.

I want my book to be an insight into the reality of living with rape, and also to be an inspiration to anyone who has suffered in this way.

≈ 1 ≈

One year on!

It's three o'clock in the morning or thereabouts. Mo's just rung. We have had yet another crazy conversation. I rolled a joint, just a weak one, whilst balancing the phone between my shoulder and my chin. When Mo rang the shop earlier today, he asked for me to send him 10 Silk Cut Purple and a couple of joints. I sent him them, a packet of cheese and onion crisps, two bananas and a Galaxy bar. Should have felt guilty really, considering he has what should be his last operation – the seventeenth in five years – tomorrow at 2pm. I felt no guilt. You see, when your son is recovering from cancer, you start to appreciate every day, every laugh and, yes, every tear. We're both alive still, just about, and getting better together – and we are about to embark on a huge adventure. Talking to people these days can be quite difficult. I wonder what people see. Is it me, John, the dog groomer; John, the dad, albeit through adoption; John, the son, brother, uncle, friend; or John, the boss? In my head, when people look at me now, they see John, the rape victim. When I look or stare into the mirror, I see John, the survivor.

When the monster raped me, he took some bits of my personality away and at the same time he created a new me. I'm still John, the dog groomer, but now people see me as the dog groomer extraordinaire. I'm still the brother, son, uncle,

1

but having survived, my love for my family is stronger than ever. I'm still the boss, but I'm now careful to keep business relationships purely professional whilst at the same time being a caring and understanding boss. Most of all, I'm still Mo's dad, although he calls me John. Talking to him at one o'clock in the morning – me a little stoned, him high on morphine – can be great fun. You see, we have no secrets. When I told him I was raped, his eyes filled up. He thought I didn't notice, and he was strong, real strong. He automatically understood that I needed strength, not tears, and most importantly, he didn't question me.

I've become quite the expert at telling people. When Sue, the witness care manager at Bolton Crown Court, told me I had an automatic right to anonymity, I giggled inside. You see, everyone who knows me or is trying to get to know me, has a right to know. They have a right to understand that I am a survivor of rape; a particularly violent rape. They don't have a right to ask me about what happened, but they do have a right to know that the person they see is a strong person who was brave or stupid enough to report the monster and to see him sent to prison for fifteen months. Yes, that's right, fifteen months. I console myself with something Duncan told me at my group meeting last Tuesday. I knew the monster had been in prison before; Gareth told me that right at the beginning of his investigations into my then serious allegation. He should not have told me, as it could have jeopardized the entire case.

I think he was trying to make me feel better at the time and I'm grateful he did, as it did make me feel better. Duncan, my therapist, knew that the monster had been in prison, and on Tuesday he told me and the group that the monster, my monster, at the time was wanted for beating someone up and stealing from them. I should not be happy that he beat someone up, but I am happy that when he gets out of prison he will be re-arrested, sent back to prison on remand this time, and will await his next trial. The irony is that he will get more time for aggravated theft than for a violent rape. Duncan was flabbergasted when I told him the monster got ten years on the Sex Offenders' Register. He said most people who rape get three years. He theorized at the group meeting that the judge had some personal experience of rape. It's a bit weird that the other guys in the group and I, thought that when your name got placed on the Sex Offenders' Register, it was there forever.

Duncan, Gareth and the lovely Gail, from St Mary's Centre for victims of rape and sexual assault, have all tried to explain the "huge" impact of being a sex offender on the register. The monster won't be able to get a job or even leave the country without permission from a judge, and he'll never be able to adopt or foster, thank God, and people living near him will have a right to ask the police about his criminal record.

I've just got off the train at Chester. It's a beautiful day. I'm having a large coffee, milk no sugar, at Carriages café bar. A lovely young girl has served me. She only sees me in front of her, dressed in black with a big bright pink scarf, a healthy glow to my skin, long, newly-styled hair and sunglasses. She got a huge smile when I thanked her for my coffee. She probably wouldn't believe that my son is awaiting the conception of three babies. Hopefully, twins from the Russian surrogate – a natural blonde with green eyes – and a single baby from the Indian surrogate. She probably would believe that my thirty-four-year-old brother is in prison in Malaga. She may struggle if I was to tell her that he is in prison for murder; not the fact that he has allegedly murdered someone, but the ease with which I would tell her. I'm finishing my coffee now and going to really test myself by going to use the loo in the station. You see, the monster has created a vulnerable adult – a grown man, a businessman, who cannot use a public toilet. But when you need to go, you need to go, so here goes. Or maybe I'll have another cig first and finish that coffee; £2.20, outrageous. Had that cig and went to the loo, it was fine. Felt sick inside but, hey, had a piss in a public loo. Some guy tried to catch my eye on the way out; he was quite cute really.

Managed to get hold of Mo, he's just about to arrive at the hospital for his op. Please let it be his last one. I nearly missed the train as I put the wrong watch on; it had stopped at 12.20. I suppose writing this, I forgot to check the time.

Now, on the 2.23, platform two from Chester to Holyhead, the train is full and my hand is aching. The weather has changed, dull and wet. Never liked Holyhead, but I wanted some "me" time, hence the train and boat and not a flight. Gavin, the other groomsman at Brian and Gill's wedding, has text me. A friend of his has died at thirty-nine, from a massive heart attack, leaving two young kids. Mark and Fatima. I didn't know him, but how tragic.

Gav's at the funeral, he's picking me up from Mum's at 11.30 tomorrow morning. Ali's driving and I'm sitting in the back of her son's disability "van" in a wheelchair, all the way from Dublin to Kilkenny – can't fucking wait! Paul's meeting us there at the Coach House Hotel. Think we are pushing it for time, though. Gav and I have to be at the tailor's first to have any last minute alterations to our suits, and we have to carry a red carpet from Brian and Gill's hotel, through the grounds of the castle, before Gill arrives for the ceremony. I've got a reading; haven't learned it, but it's only short so, although dreading it, it should be ok. Gav managed to get out of doing a reading – jammy bastard! At least Eugene has to make a speech.

I'm on the boat now, the *Jonathon Swift*; one hour forty-five minutes to Dublin. Rang Mum and Natasha, my youngest sister. She'll be waiting for me at the port; bet she's dead late. I've just text Duncan asking him to call me, not because I feel frightened or vulnerable, but because I don't know whether I can use the monster's name in this book or not. If he can't ring, I can ask him at the next group meeting – Tuesday in two weeks. At first I hated the idea of going to the group, especially when Duncan said where it was, the Quaker Hall in Manchester. Then I thought I'd quite prefer that people thought I was a camp-looking Quaker rather than a man who's been raped, even though neither Duncan nor I knew what a Quaker was. I now know what a Quaker is – misconceptions, eh? Although I still think sitting in a circle or square and staring at each other is a bit weird, I'm sure they do other stuff.

When I first arrived at the Quaker Hall – a beautiful building behind the Central Library in Manchester city centre – I sat on the steps outside; I was early. I thought I'd wait and see who went into the hall before me and play a little game to myself. "Has he or has he not been raped?" I called it. Several men walked by me and into the hall. There was no way of knowing if they had been raped or not, then I realised that the hall was used by lots of groups and organisations, so "my game was up".

It was seven in the evening. Here goes, I thought, and very nervously – but not with an episode of PTSD – I went in. The lady on reception, who I now know to be a Quaker, pointed to the room where Duncan held his group. I'd stopped at the LIDL in the Arndale for biscuits for the group. I'd prayed beforehand that there would be coffee. At previous therapy sessions with Duncan in the Lesbian and Gay Foundation or at the sessions at the lifeline centre in Oldham Street, there was no coffee. However, he did have coffee when we'd meet in a café or bar in town. There WAS tea and coffee. Rob, Graham, Gary and Simon were also survivors of childhood sexual abuse or, in one man's case, both sexual abuse and rape. A really soft spoken, gentle man, about my age or younger, had been sexually abused as a child and raped as an adult. I couldn't believe this and felt a bit of a fraud. I'd "only" been raped as an adult. That man told me I was amazing.

The group did what we call "checking in". Basically, it's a quick intro and a chat about how your life is going. For some it was just ok, for others not so ok. The group try to focus on helping each other with advice, or just by showing some basic compassion. I'd had the verdict at this stage, but wasn't back in court for another two weeks for the sentence. I left that first group meeting feeling good. I learned a very valuable lesson about pain; emotional pain. That lesson was that there is no hierarchy on pain. The impact of rape or sexual abuse on any person – man, woman or child – is very much dependent on that person.

Gareth had said that to me from the moment he walked into my life, when I first reported the monster. In his experience, as a Nightingale-trained detective, some victims hate that word "rape" but can get on with their lives almost right away, and others commit suicide, self-harm, drink or drug themselves to death, with every other form of self-destruction in between. I was determined that my life was not going to be destroyed further by the monster. I'd nearly lost my business, I'm in huge debt, but I would survive this. Duncan just rang but we couldn't hear each other; bad signal. I've text him to say I'm ok and will talk to him when I get back to Manchester.

Tash was late by ten minutes; not to worry. She had Scott, my nephew, in the car. She told me I looked great. Maybe my new hairstyle was nice. Geoff, my best friend, but now in my past, had just done it. Long and blond, I'd also dyed my eyelashes and brows, and was hoping to get a bit of a tan on the boat. The forecast said sunshine and showers. Didn't expect showers all the way. No tan then. Scott rabbited on about football, GAA and hurling. Later, he rested his head in his hands on the armchair and talked about all sorts of things; from the building of the Titanic, to being not able to swim while in Malaga in case sharks got him, to whatever kids talk about. He has new teeth now and is going to Mourne Road School next week; big school.

Mum and I are back from the pub now. We've played darts and I wasn't as good as Mum, but I did ok. We had coffee and a cig. I'm in bed now, writing this. Brian rang; he's pissed, not surprising as he's getting married in the morning. It's 4.30am; the wedding's at 3.30pm. But I've reset my clock from my normal 6am to 9.30am. It's 25th August – one year to the day. I got through it and have had a good day; the anniversary of me being raped. I hope I forget that anniversary one day.

When Brian rang me last night, Tash answered my phone as I was having a cig with Mum at the back of the Bridge House in Rialto, my family's local. Brian said to Tash, "I hope he's drinking water, he's got a reading tomorrow."

I can't sleep yet again. A dog is barking, a big one by the sounds of it. Tried to look out the Velux window in the attic room; the kids call it John's room. Scott is asleep, Dad is too, I presume, and Tash has gone for a McDonalds with her friend, Rowie. Rowie is expecting her third child and Tash her second. Babies seem to be appearing out of nowhere, Mo's

7

three are not even conceived yet. I struggle at times to explain to people about Mo, never mind the three or however many on the way.

Over coffee, Mum and I had a brief conversation about my "good news". The monster will be locked up for a long time. Not for rape but for being a monster. A twenty-year-old, good-looking, trendy, personable and believable MONSTER.

Just opened the skylight to check the weather. "Ahh, they deserve it," I thought, as it looked sunny and fine. It's Ireland, however, so never expect too much! Had a coffee, no-one up yet. Great, I can take my time getting ready. Brian had me on the phone 'til 2.30am, pissed, nervous, just wanting to chat, and having a laugh and a giggle about his nearly-finished speech. I cried inside when he got to the "most important bit". The bit when he explains that I introduced Gillian to him. We had a "man moment", a brief moment of shared emotion – him doing his best to hide it so as not to "upset" me when really he is trying to cheer me up, even though I am really quite happy right at that moment; and me suppressing that emotion as I don't want to appear ungrateful.

Head's a bit fuzzy. In a blind panic, I'm looking for my suit. Shit, my wedding suit! Where the fuck is it? Not in my suitcase, not hung up anywhere; it must be downstairs. I realise almost instantly that I'm a dickhead, again. My suit's in Kilkenny, at the tailor's. It's 9.30am, feeling a bit nervous, but it's not an episode of PTSD. Gavin should be arriving at 11.30am with Ali; not met her yet. Mo's not been in touch yet. I get ready and wait with Mum and Scott in the lounge. Gav arrives at 12 noon in a taxi.

There was an awkward atmosphere on the ten minute journey to his and Ali's house in Crumlin. Ali has a son, Zach. She's on her way back from St Michael's House, a respite residential unit for young people with severe disabilities. As the taxi drove off, Gav and I hugged briefly outside on the drive. An icebreaking moment, I believe, as from that moment we are back to ourselves, almost. We went into their nice little ex-Corporation house, with a special extension for Zach's bedroom. I had a cig in the garden and played footie with their two mongrel dogs, friendly dogs who really knew how to catch the ball. Then Ali bounced in, full of energy. She's small and petite; just had her hair done; very pretty with a beaming smile. She greeted me with a huge hug and a kiss, as I did her.

The journey down to Kilkenny began. Ali packed a great picnic basket; well, a holdall with crisps, water, lots of Red Bull, and some tasty bits and pieces. Gavin brought more clothes than both of us put together and he even remembered our matching groomsmen's brollies. Looked like we were going to need them. Just as we set off, it threw it down, but we were warm, dry and looking forward to the day ahead. It was 12.30ish and Gavin decided that he needed his hair cut before we hit the motorway. The tiny barber's shop on Sundrive Road just happened to be empty; by coincidence it was called "Gavin's barbers". Gavin went in and I went next door to the bank to change some money, then headed back to the barber's. Gavin said Ali had gone to pick up some more bits and pieces for the journey. Gavin, the barber, was quite cute, gay and really chatty. I walked in on a conversation which, as we were going to a wedding, inevitably turned to alcohol and our favourite tipples. Gavin the barber and I didn't like Guinness.

"My" Gavin did, and lots of it. Gavin the barber and I were really gay, as we both agreed Guinness was only tolerable with a drop of blackcurrant in it. Then Gavin the barber joked that as a kid, your eyes would sting if you went into the loo after your dad had used it. Gavin and I agreed, as all three of us had dads who drank Guinness by the bucket load. I joked that Plumbob, my dad, hadn't had a dry shite in twenty years but he was still here, eh? "My" Gavin's hair was nice – a little too short for my liking, but he liked it that way. Ali came back and we said our goodbyes to Gavin the barber. "Don't get too drunk," he said. "Are you fucking mad?" my Gavin said. "It's a bleeding wedding."

We headed for the motorway with Ali driving, Gavin in the passenger seat, and me in the back. Zach's wheelchair had been taken out and I actually had a car seat to sit on. Gavin directed Ali using the SatNav on his very fancy new phone. Ali struggled to get to the M50 – how could anyone not know how to get to the M50? I thought, but hey, we were on our way to my oldest friend's wedding. The traffic on the Naas Road was mad, as it always was. We were late; dead late. We spent most of the journey laughing and at times, stressing that we were not going to make it. Brian would go mad, I thought. We had to get there, pick up our suits, check into the hotel, get ready for a wedding and find Kilkenny Castle, not to mention find Paul, who was meeting us at the hotel.

We finally got to Kilkenny; there were poxy castles everywhere. Which one was it? Brian rang at 3.10pm, not stressed at all. "Just get to Langton's," he said, "pick up the suits." I hoped mine would fit. I'd emailed my measurements months ago, well before the trial, and God knows my weight had been up and down until I'd finally got back to my reassuring nine-and-a-half stone.

As we pulled up at Langton's, we saw Brian and Eugene smoking outside. They looked great in their fine suits. Eugene was Brian's best man. They'd worked offshore on the oilrigs for a while, and had lived together in Amsterdam for many, many years.

Gavin and I agreed that Gillian must have chosen the suits. I gave Brian a big hug and, as always in our very metro man relationship, we told each other that we loved each other. He gave us our suits and we drove off to find the Coach House Hotel. It was just down the road from Langton's where the wedding party were having a few drinks. We got to the Coach House, ran to our rooms – which on first sight were ok – then, as I got changed, disaster! My trousers were too big, just slightly. I was back to a twenty-eight inch waist and they were a thirty inch. Thank God Gavin had a belt; it was pretty basic but it did the job. Brian rang, "It's three thirty, for fuck's sake, where are you? We're all waiting at the castle." I rang Paul. "Where are you?" "I'm at the castle," he replied. Gavin, Ali and I rushed through the tidy antiquated and quaint streets of a buzzing Kilkenny town; the castle was only a five minute walk away. The weather had changed again – sunny and warm but a little windy. Everyone stared at the three of us in our top hats and tails, but we didn't care; we'd made it on time.

I was really nervous about my reading but strangely, I thought, no PTSD. Not a thing. Normal nerves but no need for an ambulance; now that would be embarrassing. Everyone was waiting outside in the castle grounds. They all looked great. Brian's mum, Ursula, asked Gav and I to hand out the roses for the men's lapels and the ladies' dresses. I was also charged with the duty of making sure everyone was seated in the tower before the arrival of the happy couple. It got to 4pm and I had my last cig before the ceremony then rounded everyone up. Gavin and I got everyone seated in the fairy-tale tower and waited; they were fashionably late by about ten minutes. "Here Comes the Bride" was played, and in they came.

Gillian looked beautiful in her tight-fitting cream dress –
silk or satin, I wasn't too sure. I didn't like the look on
Melissa's face. I don't think she liked her dress. Don't fucking
blame her, I thought. Bet Gill did that on purpose. The other
bridesmaid didn't look too impressed either. Where the hell
was Paul? I kept thinking. When Brian and Gill sat down, the
rest of us did too. Just as the Registrar was about to start, in
crept Paul. He did that thing people do when they arrive late
for an important meeting at work; he literally slid into a seat at
the back of the tower room.

The ceremony was really nice. Gavin did his reading then
it was my turn. I kept thinking, this is like the poxy court. I
spoke into a mic and the whole thing was filmed. The big
difference was that I wasn't behind a screen and there was no
rapist behind bulletproof glass. There was, however, a jury of
sorts – the wedding party. Not sure who was the judge. Gill, I
suppose.

I stood up and started my reading. Here goes, I thought.
Just before I started, I looked at Brian and the look he gave
me will stay with me forever. He was proud of me, like a
father watching his son in a school play. Had I really become
that vulnerable? Had the monster turned me into someone I
didn't want to be, or even like? I started the reading, *The
Apache Wedding Blessing*. "Now each of you will feel no rain, for
each of you will be shelter to the other, now you will feel no
cold, for each of you will be warmth to the other. Now you
are two persons, but there is only one life before you. May
beauty surround you both in the journey ahead and through
all the years. May happiness be your companion, and your
days together be good and long upon the earth. Your
adventure has just begun."

I'd done it. My reading was done and, like everyone, I got
a round of applause. When the Registrar said, "You may kiss

the bride", I cried. I was so happy for them; my best friend and the beautiful lady I had introduced to him.

I'd met Gill when we both started working at a recruitment agency in Tallaght. She had met the old me; confident, funny and one of, if not the best, sales people in that office. I spent ages trying to get her and Brian together but I really didn't think they would ever get married. But here we were at the wedding.

After the customary, if not a little too many, photographs, Gav, Ali, Paul and I headed back to the hotel to change. I decided to keep my suit on. Paul somehow had driven to Kildare and not Kilkenny and that's why he was late, the dickhead. We had a couple of drinks at the bar before heading off to Langton's. Before I left Dublin, Plumbob had said to mention him to the owner. At the time I had thought, "Stop showing off, Dad." We got to Langton's at 5pm that afternoon and were seated in a beautiful function room. The meal was delicious; three courses of fine food with complimentary wine and champagne. I didn't taste the champagne but everyone said it was nice. The owner of Langton's personally went round to each and every table introducing himself and generally being a great host. When he got to our table, I asked him if he knew Joe Lennon. "Plumbob?" he replied. "Of course I know him. Sure, doesn't the whole of Ireland know Plumbob Lennon?" So Dad wasn't showing off, after all.

The day became evening and the most important part of the day began: the speeches. Brian spoke about Gill and, of course, thanked me for introducing her to him. Ursula spoke all about Brian and her memories of "Big Brian", who'd tragically and unexpectedly died the previous year. Then the big one, the Best Man's speech. Eugene went on and on and on and on and... Well, you get the point. He was, however, hilarious and Brian and I both agreed that it was best I didn't do a speech. We both knew it would have been too much so soon after the court case.

We danced the night away before I asked Paul if he was ready for bed. Of course, as ever, Paul was eager to get to bed. For him it was a night of passion, for me it was to prove to myself that I could actually make love and not just go through the motions of sex. Paul and I thanked everyone for a great day and said our goodbyes. Just as we were walking towards the exit, we both tripped simultaneously and fell to the floor like two drunken fools. Everyone laughed, including us. We jumped up, dusted ourselves down, and off we went back to the Coach House.

After a couple of drinks in the hotel bar, Paul and I went to our room. The last time we'd made love – and during twenty-five years of knowing Paul, there had been many times – he had said I was distant. He should have said it was like making love to a board, but I don't think he wanted to hurt my feelings. That was back in February when I left the old shop and moved to Newton Heath. I'd not had any sexual contact with anyone since the rape. On that occasion, I'd been conscious that I was crap in bed, but I knew Paul hadn't thought about, and should never have been expected to think about, sex being a major trigger for my PTSD. It was now August, so I was hoping that I could make love like I used to; with passion, energy and enthusiasm.

We got undressed and I got into bed whilst Paul freshened up in the bathroom. He put the light out and climbed in beside me. We caressed and explored each other's bodies with the gentlest of hands. Paul leaned towards me and we kissed, gently at first then passionately, until he jumped up and puked all over the place.

So much for my psychosexual experiment! And obviously a good shag was right out of the question. We fell asleep after that and made up for our passionless night the following morning. I'd proved that I could make love again and enjoy it and, probably more importantly to me, Paul enjoyed it too. Later I would explain to Duncan the huge importance of my love-making. "Wow!" he said. "So soon?" Here I was, at a therapy session, explaining a night of passion when I've probably had more pricks than Kerplunk.

≈ 2 ≈

The Road to Recovery

We met up with the others late that morning. We all nursed our hangovers with coffee and went for lunch in a really trendy wine bar. Over lunch, Brian announced to everyone at our table that I was writing a book. Fuck! I thought. Why have you done that? One of his cousins from Australia said, "Oh brilliant, what's it about?" Here goes, I thought, I'd better get used to this. So I promptly replied, "Rape." She nearly choked on her Caesar salad, gulped the mouthful she was eating down, composed herself, and said gently, "Can I ask why?" "Because I was raped," I calmly replied.

Gavin interjected very quickly, "So how is it going with the book, John?" I told him, and the others, that it was early days but that I was trying to make it funny in parts. "How can you find any humour in that?" Gavin said. "I suppose I'll have to try," I replied.

We had our lunch and then it was time to say our goodbyes. Paul headed back to Cavan and Ali drove us back to Dublin. I spent the following day enjoying my family's company, and in particular spending time with the kids. Mum and I went to the pub, but I only had a couple as I didn't want to be dying on the journey home. Before I went to bed that night, I did what I normally did on a trip home, I popped my

16

head into Dad's room. And even though he was asleep, I kissed my dad on his forehead and whispered, "I love you."

The following morning I got ready and had breakfast and coffee with Mum. She made a full Irish, with proper white pudding and real Irish recipe sausages.

Time to go back to my little shop and my life in Manchester. Before saying goodbye, I showed Mum the beautiful silver lighter Brian and Gillian had given me. "It's gorgeous," she said. I would later give that lighter to Wayne, his first Christmas pressie from me as he passed the time in that awful prison.

Time to go. Mum and I hugged at the door, and off I went to catch the Luas, Dublin's tram, into town. Just before I left, Scott came down to say goodbye. I hugged him nearly to death and told him to give Dad a kiss from me when he eventually got out of bed.

My other sister, Michelle, rang to say goodbye as I was getting off the Luas. She said she would try to get over for a weekend soon, maybe bringing Roy, her youngest, with her. I hadn't seen Roy on this trip. He must be tall now and I knew he was still football mad; a great kid, like all of them, I suppose. My brother, Paul, had offered me a lift to Dublin Port, but I wanted to get the Luas, have a nice walk through Dublin city centre and get the bus from Busaras to the Port. I waited at Busaras for nearly an hour.

I decided to check out my personal vulnerability levels, so off I went to the filthy loos. Yet again, I was fine. At the bus station, I said hello to the pretty Malaysian lady I'd given directions to in Manchester. She told me Dublin was beautiful and that I was "sweet". I also watched a rucksack for a lady from London, while she went to buy some water from the kiosk. She had been away for ten days, during the riots in the UK. She was from Tottenham, where it all started.

We talked about the world of social work, as we had similar work backgrounds, and we put that world to rights. We spoke quite a bit about the riots and the kind of people that took part. We also chatted about justice, or the lack of it, under the direction of Kenneth Clarke. I wondered how the two men who tried to incite the riots on Facebook got four years apiece in prison, and yet other thugs who burned down buildings, etc. got weeks or months in jail. Deep down I wanted to tell that lady that the man who violently raped and beat me got fifteen months, but I didn't. If I had had the letter I wrote to Kenneth Clarke on me, I would have shown it to her. This is that very letter, to which I never received a reply.

Att: Mr Kenneth Clarke

From: John Lennon

Ref: Proposals to reduce sentences of rapists and other criminals.

Dear Mr Clarke,

My name is John Lennon. I live in Blackley, Manchester above my small business, a Dog Grooming Salon. I employ Sarah full time and a host of other Saturday helpers. My business is doing well and it continues to grow. This always amazes me, as the business has been moved already in the year-and-a-half that it has been in existence.

You see, Mr Clarke, I was raped by a stranger on 25 August last year in the flat above my old shop in Prestwich, Manchester. I was violently and viciously raped. I thought I was going to die. I have received an email from Gareth, the officer I first told. He has kindly typed up my Victim Impact Statement and has sent me a copy. Please find that attached. I have also sent you a copy of a statement from Duncan Craig, of Survivors Manchester, who did a press release on the day he heard about your damaging proposals.

Duncan is also my therapist, I don't see him that often as I feel I am getting better; most days are ok now but I still have the panic disorder which can require hospitalization. The Beta Blockers the doctors prescribed help on a bad day but I really don't want to take them unless absolutely necessary.

*My trust in people is getting better and I even go out on occasion. Mr Clarke, my attacker's trial is on 27*th *June, I give evidence on the 28*th *and the other witnesses after that.*

As the Justice Minister, you should have a very clear and real understanding of crime, all crime; not gained through personal experience of course, but an understanding of the impact crime, and in particular rape, has on the victim. You do not. Please resign, Mr Clarke, and give hope to all survivors of rape – male, female, young and old.

Thank you for reading this.

Kindest Regards,

Mr John Lennon.

Duncan had also written a press release in response to Mr Clarke's ludicrous proposals for sentence reductions. I would have shown that to this lady, too, had I had it to hand. It reads:

Press Statement

Wednesday, 18 May 2011: 22.30hrs

Today in an interview with BBC Radio 5 Live, the Justice Secretary, Rt. Hon Kenneth Clarke, rejected the notion that "rape is rape" in saying "*No, it is not.*"

Mr Clarke stated: "*date rape can be as serious as the worst rapes…*"

<u>Survivors Manchester strongly condemns Mr Clarke's comments and publicly maintains that rape is a serious and devastating crime, affecting both females and males equally.</u> Addressing the Commons today, Labour Leader Ed Milliband stated the Justice Secretary *"cannot speak for women of this country"*.

<u>Survivors Manchester would like to publicly remind Mr Miliiband that males are also victims of rape.</u>

Duncan Craig, Founder and Service Director for Survivors Manchester, stated: *"We work tirelessly to support adult male survivors of childhood sexual abuse and rape in the Greater Manchester area and are one of only a few organisations across the UK specifically supporting males. Irresponsible comments like those made today not only cause upset and hurt, but can often keep male victims silent and prevent them from coming forward."*

Having recently been rejected by the Ministry of Justice for much needed funding to continue delivering front line services, Survivors Manchester demands that Parliament recognises:

- Rape IS Rape;
- Men ARE victims; and
- Victims and survivors of all forms of sexual violence should be given access to specialist support in order to regain control of and move forward in their lives.

Survivors Manchester has directly supported 120 adult male survivors of sexual abuse and rape; over 50 professionals, partners and family members; and 10 women wanting signposting to female specific services. Since 2009, demand on the service has grown 7% per year. On average, Survivors Manchester has actively supported 10 individual victims per month, 90% of whom access face-to-face services. However, since January 2011, the organisation is now directly supporting 19 individuals per month, an increase of 90% on 2010!

End.

For further information please contact:

Duncan Craig, Survivors Manchester Service Director, on 0xxxxxxxx or duncan@survivorsmanchester.org.uk

I obviously didn't show these letters to this lady, but we both agreed that the British justice system was fucked. I stood before this lady, whose ex-girlfriend was a dog groomer, a well-groomed, God-knows-what age, blond, blue-eyed man. I was finally not the raped man but just a guy on his way home to Manchester.

I'm on the ferry now. It's been a nice trip so far. The Malaysian lady sitting at the table next to me has just woken up. We are getting off soon. The Tannoy woke her and she immediately started reading her book. Must be a bloody good read, I'm thinking. The really quiet country guy beside me has put his laptop and computer magazine into his holdall. I get the impression he is going for work or maybe an interview in the UK. Been there myself, you see, and kinda recognise the signs. Went on deck about twenty minutes ago for a cig. I text Mo to see if he wanted me to bring him anything when I got back to Manchester. He text back, "I'm sore, really sore, never been like this. Send some chocolate and a few joints, but make them stronger than the last, they help with the pain. Thanks."

I got to Piccadilly at 9.45pm and almost ran to the shop to get Mo some bits and pieces. He's in so much pain, I feel his pain and need to feel that pain. It's Mardi Gras weekend; there are pissed-up gay people everywhere. The shop assistant asked if I'd had a good weekend. I think he thought I was here for Mardi Gras and on my way home. I caught the tram home and when I got in, I called Newco taxis. I would only use them when I had to get a taxi to court; somehow I felt safe with them. When the taxi arrived, I asked the driver to take the goodies I had bought to Mo in the Skyline building on Rochdale Road. I hid a couple of joints in an empty cig packet, hopefully they would help with the pain. I'm now ready for bed.

≈ 3 ≈

My Baby Brother

J ust woke up, it's Tuesday. Called Lee. He said Saturday had been busy. Lee's not been working here long. On his first day, I asked him to come upstairs after work, there was something I needed to explain to him – my PTSD, and of course the reason why I had this lifelong disorder. I needed to explain this to him just in case I had an episode at work and he needed to call the ambulance. Lee's reaction was brilliant; he fought the tears in his eyes and gave me strength. I felt safe working with Lee and could see us becoming great friends.

Just had a call from Kerry. Indie went for a walk off-lead with her boyfriend, Andrew. I can't believe it. Fair play to you, Andrew.

The day came and went and Indie and I have just had dinner. I've been thinking a lot about my trip to Ireland. It has sorted a lot of things out for me but, probably most importantly for me, I now know I can use a public loo. Just before I went to sleep, Mo rang. It turns out our "mad" conversations are not so mad, after all. I've just read him the first page of my book, my "Journey To Justice?" He said the tag line should read "and a tramp in between". We laughed so loud it's silly.

Some time later

Spoke to Pearl twice last night. Everyone is fine in Malaga, Wayne is still on remand for first degree murder. When the newspapers wrote what they did, no-one – including me – ever believed a word of it. Here is one of the articles written in the Irish *Sunday World*.

"Freddie pal nabbed for Spain killing

A CLOSE pal of mob bosses Fat Freddie xxxxxx and Brian xxxxxx has been arrested in Spain for the "Reservoir Dogs" style murder of a British man. The *Sunday World* has learned that 35-year-old Wayne "Blinkey" Lennon, from Dolphin's Barn in Dublin, is in a Spanish jail while cops investigate the gruesome torture and slaying of Paul xxxxx. xxxxx (32), had his ear hacked off in a scene similar to the famous Quentin Tarantino film and died of head injuries and massive blood loss. He was killed after he opened the door of his apartment in Benalmadena at around 11am on April 21, 2010. Spanish police say that Blinkey Lennon and fellow Dubliner, Brian xxxxxx, burst into the apartment and that one of the men pulled a knife from the kitchen drawer. It is alleged that one of the pair held xxxxx's girlfriend and she watched helplessly as his earlobe was hacked off and he was slashed across the nose. The knife was then twice plunged deep into his chest. xxxxx collapsed violently to the floor as the two men fled. His terrified girlfriend was so shocked by the murder that she also ran out of the apartment. Detectives eventually managed to track her down and she identified Lennon and xxxxx as being responsible for the stabbing. They raided the flat where Lennon was staying and found blood-stained clothes that are believed to have belonged to the victim. Both of the suspects disappeared but Lennon was finally arrested in Gran Canaria on May 7 of this year but details of his arrest have only emerged now. It is unclear if xxxxxx is also in custody."

That article could not have got things more wrong. As a family, and to everyone who knew the truth, we knew that it was full of mistakes and we even considered suing that newspaper. Maybe that day will come, I thought.

Pearl told me lots about Dad's birthday party. Everyone had gone over to Malaga and Pearl put on a great party in her little bar for Dad's seventieth and Paul Kelly, Michelle's husband, who was fifty. The party went well, but Pearl seemed a little put out that nobody had helped her with the preparations.

I couldn't go because of work and, to be honest, I couldn't afford it, what with the trip to Ireland and the usual bills. But hey, there would be many more parties! Apparently Dad and his friend, Stephen O'Driscoll, went to one of the largest rave clubs in the Costa Del Crime. I laughed at the thought of it, but deep down I was really proud of Dad and said to myself, "I hope I'm doing that at seventy."

My other sister, Dawn, called me from London. I hadn't spoken to her since before the rape but she was planning a trip to Manchester to see her son, Dean Adam, who was now twenty-three years old and lived and worked in Manchester. I told Dawn she, her other son, Lorenzo, and their dog, Paddy, were welcome to stay with me. I was really looking forward to seeing them.

It's now 10pm and I have had a particularly bad day. I managed to work, Lee was late again, and the shop was busy. My anxiety level was really on high alert and I couldn't understand why. It's been this way for a few days now and I've spent today working it out.

I have started sleeping on the couch again. After the rape, I slept on the couch in the living room for weeks. When I moved to Newton Heath, I brought that bed – the bed where it happened – to the little flat, but I never slept in that bed; I gave that bed to Sarah. However, I've now got a beautiful new flat and a beautiful new bed. I'm determined to sleep in my new bed.

In bed now, I'm surrounded by my very fancy wrought iron bedroom furniture. I bought a mattress from a man in a van for £120 but it should have been £1300, so why can't I sleep?

I've worked it out! My anxiety disorder, my PTSD, is not only about anxiety when remembering what happened to me; it's about any anxiety. I've learned new breathing techniques and am proud to say that I am actually controlling this disorder rather than it controlling me. I'll try to sleep now in my fancy bed, with my very expensive – albeit robbed – mattress.

I actually managed to get some sleep last night. It's 6.45am and in writing this book I've realised that I'm trying to make sense of my anger. My anger at the monster and indeed at this judicial system, and in particular Kenneth Clarke. I'll check the mail yet again to see if he has had the decency to reply to my letter.

No letter from Mr Clarke today. I'm considering whether to write to David Cameron or not; wonder would he reply to me? That's it, I'm writing to David Cameron.

Dear Mr Cameron,

My name is John Lennon. I am Irish, forty-two years old almost, an adoptive parent of a fantastic son, his name is Mo and he is of Pakistani origin. I have a great family and great friends. I run a small business in Manchester employing one young lady full time. She is also a ten per cent owner of the business, earned through her dedication and hard work.

Mr Cameron, I am also a victim of rape. I emailed Mr Kenneth Clarke over a week ago and have had no reply. I attach the documents I sent to Mr Clarke for your perusal.

Thank you in advance for reading this email and its attachments.

Kindest Regards,
Mr John Lennon

I sent this letter in July. It's now October and I've still not had a response. I, like many people, am becoming more and more dissatisfied with David Cameron's government. I've never voted in this country, but at the next general election I certainly will be voting; voting to get rid of Cameron and his cronies.

The following day

In work now, Lee's just got here. I called Gail at St Mary's a minute ago; we are to meet up this week. I had to explain to Lee who Gail was. He understood how important it was for me to see her. Gail was my Independent Sexual Violence Advisor or ISVA. After the rape, Gareth, the detective in charge of the case, recommended I go to St Mary's Centre for victims of rape and sexual assault. My forensic examination had taken place at North Manchester General Hospital, but St Mary's did much more than that. They offered counselling and, most importantly to me, they provided Gail to support me through every minute of the court case.

When I first went to St Mary's, I was scared and I hesitated outside this huge hospital before going in. I had no idea where I was going and prayed to God that there would be signs, but my dilemma was that I didn't want to see any signs like, "All rape victims go this way." Imagine. You see, I didn't want anyone to know I was a victim of such a heinous crime and I suppose, looking back, that I must have felt some shame even though my biggest issue now is trying to understand why victims feel shame. I, like other victims or survivors, didn't rape myself.

The old St Mary's Centre was located at the end of a very long, dark corridor. The first time I walked down that corridor I felt like saying, turn the poxy lights on, for fuck's sake. Gail later told me it was because of cutbacks that the lights were off during the day. I was also fully aware that I didn't feel safe walking down that long, dimly lit, empty corridor.

When I got to the end, there was an intercom system on the door. The sign said, "Please ring bell and wait in the seating area." Here I was, afraid to leave the house and, after finally finding the courage to get to a centre designed for victims of rape, I was made to wait outside in a dark corridor.

Gail came to the door. She was friendly but had a sense of strength about her. I wouldn't like to get on the wrong side of her, I thought. We went in and, after another wait in another waiting area – a bit more like a doctor's surgery this time – Gail came back with coffee and asked me to come to a counselling room with her. I went into the little room and we started to chat. This was at a time when I could not hear the word rape. I couldn't bear it, and grimaced every time she used that word.

Gail noticed this and told me I would have to get used to it as it would be used many, many times if the case got to the Crown Court, which eventually it did. One of the things that put me off Gail was what she later denied saying. At that meeting she said, "I know what you are going through." I asked myself, had she been raped? I decided to let her insensitivity go over my head; she had not been raped and therefore had no clue what I was going through. Gail and I became quite close as the months went on, and now I have nothing but complete respect and admiration for her and the people at St Mary's.

I am glad, however, that the centre has moved to a new location within the hospital. There is no long, dark corridor and the centre is bright and cheerful. On my second visit to the old centre, I waited in the waiting area. It was really quiet and I just sat there wondering why the hell I was there in the first place, and flicking through an *OK* magazine. The bell rang and the lady on reception went to the door.

In came a lady about my age. She was very distraught and was being comforted by another lady who, on first appearance, looked like her sister. They sat in the chairs next to me. Every now and then the lady who was upset would look in my direction and her eyes would fill with fear. I later explained to Gail that in my opinion, male and female victims should be treated separately. I scared that lady further, simply by being a man in her immediate proximity.

Gail told me today that she would be arranging a pre-court visit and to ask Sarah and Yvonne if they would like to come with us, or have separate visits of their own to prepare them for court.

Lee and I got on with the day. We cleaned the windows and anything else that needed cleaning, including Indie. Paul rang in the morning. I passed the phone to Lee, who chatted with Paul for a bit. When Lee handed the phone back to me, Paul said Lee sounded sexy. I wonder even now, can a person sound sexy over the phone?

Lee and I groomed a few dogs and the day came and went.

I'm writing this in the evening before bed, and hoping that I can stick with my new routine of actually sleeping in a bed. It seems less important to sleep, but just being in a bed – either awake or asleep – is important to me and something I'm working really hard at doing.

1.44 am. Just woke up. Indie gets confused with my sleeping patterns. Does she need to go out?

She did. She now wants something to eat – raw or cooked chicken. Fuck that, it's 2am, she can wait till tomorrow. When I was in Ireland, Kerry and Andrew said she was just perfect. Somebody had to be lying; she's a nightmare. She pulls on the lead, but not too much on the harness; she won't eat, not till she's ready, which means chicken or whatever meat I give her can be left hidden in the house for hours until I find where she's hidden it. She's stopped washing her meat in the water bowl. Just check if she needs water. No, that's ok.

I think she wants me to sleep on the couch. Well, I'm not. I think I'm in danger of turning into one of those "my dog's my baby" head wrecks. People know generally that my attitude to these people – probably a large percentage of my customers, but not large enough to make me give up dog grooming – is that I tolerate them. I'm not one of them.

When they say that they have "rescued" a dog, I usually joke to whoever's listening that they didn't run across hot desert sands, they didn't swing through the trees like Tarzan, or swim through a shark-infested sea. They generally went to Manchester Dogs' Home, paid £80 or whatever, and bought a dog. They seem to think, however, that by relaying a story of their dog's "abuse" at every opportunity, it makes them special or even better than the person – like me – who chose the breed they wanted and paid the big money; in my case £750 for Indie.

These people really are the joke, and I and whoever works with me have to listen to them, day in and day out! "We think that's a cig burn." "He must have been beaten." "She was starved half to death and left on a motorway." "He was kicked black and blue." "He'll only eat human food as he was fed on scraps." "If you put the light on suddenly he shakes, he must have been beaten in the dark." The shit I listen to in this job! Thank God for the normal owners.

If they only knew what I know about Indie. She was beaten and abused in her attempts to protect me from the monster, but she's now a well-rounded dog – well, wolf hybrid – with a great personality, who loves life and all it has to offer.

Later I was to write an article for the *Dogs Today* magazine about Indie and how we helped each other in our recovery. Indie, you see, suffers with her own form of PTSD. This is the article that featured in *Dogs Today* and would later lead to her receiving one of only five Endal Awards at the London Pet Show 2012.

≈ 4 ≈

A Dog's Life

Indie's Road to Recovery

I'm John Lennon, a Dog Groomer from Dublin. I've worked with animals most, but not all, of my life. I qualified from Manchester Medical School, Dept. of Biological Sciences, in 1992 as an Animal Technician. I've taught Animal Care at BTEC and NVQ levels 1-3 and hold NVQ Assessors Awards D32 and D33 plus Internal Verifiers Award D34. I worked in UMIST and have had various Vet Nurse jobs in between. Jonathon and I opened our first, and only, pet shop and dog grooming salon in the 90s, and somehow I became a social worker between then and now, but returned to dog grooming full time several years ago.

I'm writing a book called, "My Journey to Justice?" My book is about me and the impact my experience has had on me, my family and friends, and indeed, Indie. Indie is due her puppies on 8th February, but that date could obviously change. I have a small business in Blackley, Manchester.

Jodie asked me to try to explain my and Indie's road to recovery, but that is impossible. My recovery is complete. I still have Post Traumatic Stress Disorder but I have learned to manage this on a daily basis. I was helped most by an organisation called Survivors Manchester and, in particular, my therapist. Duncan. "Survivors" is a small charity that helps male adult survivors of childhood sexual abuse and rape and in some cases both. I also received great help from DCI Gareth J. of Bury Police and Gail Morgan from St Mary's Centre for Victims of Rape and Sexual Assault. I don't feel a need to tell the world how much support I got from my friends and my wonderful family, but that support was there in its many shapes and forms.

It was a Friday evening. Geoff drove Tex, my 13-year-old Northern Inuit and I, to the vet's, where we met Yvonne. The vet got the dose wrong and it took 35 minutes for my beloved noble friend to die. I don't remember much after that. Tex was gone.

I waited for two months before deciding to get another Inuit and fostered Mas, then Sammy. Mas, another Inuit, ended up with Sarah, my then assistant; he's doing just fine now, as far as I know. Sammy, an Elkhound, went to my sister, Linda. I see her often and, although still a challenge, she's a great little dog.

I decided to finally take the plunge and went to buy Indie, my beautiful Indie. I drove and Yvonne came with me. I'd never been to the breeder's house but had heard lots of tales about her on the Inuit circuit. Indie was there, shy but obviously clever. There were two sibling bitches remaining and they were not my cup of tea; one was black and white with a short coat, and the other was just like Indie but again with a short coat. They were very loud and attention-seeking so, against Yvonne's advice, I chose Indie.

She was, in my opinion, the best of the three. She was timid and nervous and had no idea about play or interaction with me. After a few days of her settling in to this new and very crazy dog groomer's world, she retreated into herself. I even considered taking her back to the breeder. I suppose I was comparing her to Tex, but she could not be more different. Indie is Indie, and Tex was perfect but different.

Maybe I had forgotten what it was like to have a puppy. She sure reminded me, but after a lot of off-lead walking in Heaton Park, she came round and before long she was a happy and playful puppy.

My dog grooming business was busy and Indie learned lots of good, and sometimes bad, habits from the customers' dogs; all sizes, shapes and temperaments.

It was the 22nd of August and Indie and I met a group of friends in the Gay Village. I was to enter her into the Pink dog show.

Indie was 26 weeks old and pretty; really pretty. I asked a man I had just met to parade her up and down in front of the large crowd. That man introduced me as his boyfriend, but we had only met the day before.

We had a great time at the dog show, but the new man in my life – my monster – would not go home. I tried politely, and not so politely, to tell him to go but he just wouldn't. Indie took an instant dislike to the monster.

The night before he decided to viciously and callously rape me, Yvonne came round for dinner. The monster cooked jerk chicken and rice and said it was his goodbye treat for me as he would be going back to his flat the following day.

The following morning, at 6.30am, Indie and I lay in bed with the monster. Great, I thought, he's going. But this good-looking, 20-year-old, well-spoken Jamaican man made a decision that would change his life forever. Indie was present when the monster raped me and she tried everything in her power to stop him. She could not stop him; neither could I.

He got sent to prison many months later and will be on the Sex Offenders' Register for ten years.

We moved both business and home, as I lived above the old shop. Indie and I got a flat in Newton Heath, which had a large African population. Indie found this particularly difficult. She regularly growled, or worse, at my neighbours.

She has gone through most of the stages of trauma, including disassociation through environmental change, huge changes in exercise patterns, toilet training gone mad, major food issues, a fear of kitchens and bathrooms, and lots of strange behaviours in between, such as staring at the floor in the corners of rooms for anything up to an hour at a time.

We got better together through many processes and techniques – many I had no idea about, others I was very conscious of. I used over-exposure to black people and carefully managed introductions to friends and family with dark skin. I also took advice from many people, with my assistant, Kerry, having a big influence on many of the decisions I made.

After completing her Animal Management Course with distinction, Kerry is now studying Animal Behaviour at Manchester University. My small, but dedicated, team at "The Park" have all helped with Indie.

Lee has become a huge help to both Indie and me, and has a place firmly in our pack. I'm getting on with my life, business is good, and everyone's dead excited about Indie's first litter of puppies. Life has not quite returned to normal, but we are getting better.

The photograph that accompanies this article was taken by two very special and caring people; Ken and Phil. Ken teaches people over 50 – at the College of the Third Age – the beauty of photography with the hope, I know, of inspiring them to "be inspired".

They photographed Indie and I in a very special place, the temple in Heaton Park – the highest point in Manchester; the place we ran to after our ordeal. I hope our story helps someone and their dog going through any form of trauma.

When I wrote this article, I made it really clear they were to use the word "assault" and not "rape". This was so that people of all ages, and in particular the children in my life, could read about John and Indie in the magazine. Unfortunately they used the word rape. The editor said it was a big mistake and could not apologise enough. I told her and everybody else that no child should have to understand that word and that no adult should have to explain that word to a child. She agreed, and by way of an apology she nominated Indie and me for the award at the London Pet Show, which we attended the following May.

The show was huge. I'd never been to Earl's Court Stadium and was not expecting the huge crowds who attended, many to see Indie and me. Although I was surrounded by friends and family, not to mention the thousands of people in the audience, it was Lee who came up with me and Indie to receive our prizes.

I was the third to be called up and just before we walked up, the editor read out a very brief synopsis of our story. She was very careful not to use the word rape; she used serious assault instead.

I started to fill up at the realisation of what I was about to do and Lee, who had handled Jaya all day, said to me, "Do you need me to go up with you?" I didn't say yes, I just smiled at him with tears in my eyes.

Lee, Jaya, Indie and I proudly received our prize. Alan, from Hounds for Heroes, handed me Indie's medal and we later got a three month supply of really expensive dog food. We also got a signed print of the dog version of the painting "Scream". It's called "The Howler". Imagine giving me, a rape victim, who works with dogs, that image! It's funny really, but most importantly we got Indie's medal for bravery.

In the following month's edition of *Dogs Today*, they featured Indie and I and the other four award winners.

Yoda

Caroline was struck down with ME at just seventeen. She was about to go for an interview at Liverpool Institute of Performing Arts. Before then, she had been the life and soul of everyone's party. Diagnosis was a long time coming and she felt completely isolated and spent most of her time asleep.

Caroline also became more and more anxious about going out. But in March 2011, she summoned all her bravery and went to Crufts. And although the day was completely exhausting and much of the time was spent sitting and resting, she found the French Bulldog and fell in love.

Caroline spent the next couple of months researching the breed and breeders. She found Yoda, and they have been completely inseparable ever since.

"He gives me a reason to get out of bed. Even when I have no energy, he sits with me and keeps me company and he even gives me the courage and opportunity to try new things, even if it's just a short walk to the park where he makes human friends who talk to me.

"Yoda is a little bundle of fun and joy who makes me smile even on our darkest days."

Edward

Graham Waspe got his first guide dog, called Edward, in 2004. Edward soon became quite a local favourite as he guided Graham through Stowmarket, Suffolk and went along with Graham and his wife, Sandra, to hundreds of guide dog talks and fundraising events.

In April 2010, Edward was diagnosed with a very rare form of glaucoma and the wonderful vets at the small animal clinic in Newmarket fought to save his sight. But sadly, in 2010 Edward had to have both his eyes removed.

Many tears were shed but Edward adapted well to blindness and continued to go to the guide dog talks and clearly continued to love meeting people and being out and about, just as he did when he was sighted.

Edward has warmly accepted Graham's new guide dog, Opal. Edward inspired two of the staff of the local Specsavers in Stowmarket to do a sky-dive to raise funds to train and name a new guide dog, and they called it Edward after their local celebrity. Their bosses matched their fundraising and a total of £5,088 was raised. Edward, Opal, Graham and Sandra Waspe and the Stowmarket branch continue to raise funds for little Edward's on-going training.

Edward transformed the life of Graham and has won the hearts of people worldwide with the tragic story of his sight loss, thereby also helping to raise the profile of Guide Dogs for the Blind.

Tansy

A two-year-old Cardigan Corgi had a difficult time giving birth to her first litter and some of her own pups sadly hadn't made it. Those that did survive went on to thrive and when they were five weeks old, owner Jo Lovell heard that there was another Corgi mum who was very poorly and that a litter of pups was in danger. So she volunteered young Tansy to help.

Tansy was a house pet, not a kennel dog, so the prospect of leaving her own pups to go and nurse this new litter seemed daunting, but as soon as she saw the litter of tiny pups she washed each one and sat down to feed them. She reared them all and saved their lives. Jo explains that Tansy was special for another reason.

"We had bought Tansy to help out our youngest son who was having issues at school, and who wanted a dog he could walk himself. Tansy helped him a lot, especially when it came to light that Owen was being bullied and he needed a friend who didn't judge."

Bumble

Demi Louise Shakespeare has cerebral palsy and is wheelchair-bound. Her life has been transformed since she got Bumble from Dogs for the Disabled. Demi says, "As a result of my beautiful Bumble being on hand to help, I no longer have to ask my mum or others. Knowing this puts the biggest smile on my face, because I always got upset at having to ask for assistance.

"I now have someone who not only makes me feel so happy all of the time, but she is also my best friend. The love that we have for each other is unconditional. She is the centre of attention, as we are not able to go out without someone asking what she does to help me. Confidence is something I lacked, but now I will talk to anyone. I am in my first year of university, something I couldn't have contemplated without Bumble.

"In a short period of time, we have achieved so much together. One of the many experiences we have had is appearing on BBC1's *Search For Dorothy*, as Bumble auditioned to play the role of Toto, where she got to the final ten. I entered because I knew how much she would enjoy being in the limelight. I wanted to show the world how talented my little princess and best friend was.

"Dogs for the Disabled put so much time and effort into working with dogs like Bumble. They have given me a gift that no-one else could, the best friend that any girl could ask for. Thank you."

The last to be written about was Indie. Maybe the editor thought it was best to leave the best 'til last, or maybe her editorial team wanted to promote the expensive dog food that "our" story and our very glamorous picture, taken by Phil and Ken at the temple in Heaton Park, was in fact promoting. There were pictures of this dog food under our story. It read...

Indie

John Lennon is a dog groomer from Dublin. He had not long opened a new salon in Manchester when an acquaintance, who had taken a shine to John's Northern Inuit pup, did something terrible that would change all their lives forever.

John lived above the shop and this man refused to leave, and subjected John to an horrific, vicious attack that put that man in jail. Puppy Indie did everything she could to defend her master, but she couldn't. John and Indie both suffered post-traumatic stress disorder and their lives were turned upside down. They relocated to make a fresh start, but Indie was now very wary of any young black men and obviously associated them with John's attacker.

Concentrating on getting Indie to overcome her fears and prejudices, he helped Indie and she helped him to recover too, and together they tried to get through this very upsetting period of their lives.

"We got better together," John said. "Many people have asked me, 'Did Indie save your life?' Some ask, 'Did I save Indie's?' The answer is not so clear cut. Indie was just a little puppy, she hadn't got the physical strength to intervene even though she did try. I suppose when I heard her scream from the pain of a brutal kick from the monster, that really was my trigger to find the strength from somewhere, to kick the monster away and run; run as fast as I possibly could with Indie in my arms. So the answer is twofold, we saved each other.

"In September 2012, I re-homed Indie. One of the hardest things I have ever done. She not only became a good mum, she became the mother from hell. No other dog could approach Jaya and, with a grooming business to run, I had no option other than to find her the best home possible. In came Mandy and her wonderful family.

"Linda had lots of problems with Sammy, the Elkhound I'd given her. Sammy had to go though because, after complaints about her barking and visits from the council, I found her a new home in Newcastle. The same day Mandy came for Indie; my Indie, my protector. How the fuck had this happened?

"I sat in the kitchen waiting for Sammy's new owner to come, he'd sent a driver and later I was to report him to the police for harassment. He checked on Sammy a hundred times a fucking day and I had had enough. I didn't need to know whether she was sleeping or not every two minutes, so the police did their usual thing of over protecting me and warned him off.

"Mandy came with her two sons. Mandy has kept me informed of Indie's progress, every step of the way. Indie is doing just fine in her new home."

When Tex died the previous April, I thought no dog could replace him. He was thirteen years old, my faithful friend and a giant of a dog/wolf hybrid. He was, however, kind and gentle. In the weeks leading up to his euthanasia, we didn't have many walks as his back legs would cave in. He did, however, enjoy long drives in my big old jeep. We would drive around the city and he would hang his head out of the window.

Then one day, the very strangest thing happened. I got sick of listening to the radio and found the one and only CD I had in the jeep, Boyzone, *"No Matter What"*. I loved this song and it holds a kinda poignancy for me. Malley's sister, Christine, had died several years earlier. She was a singer and had a beautiful voice. As she knew she was dying, she carefully planned her funeral. And as her coffin was removed from the church, *"No Matter What"* was played.

I put the CD on and it played several times. Tex seemed really relaxed listening to the music, but I got fed up with it and turned the radio on. Suddenly Tex became panicky and I assumed his legs were hurting. I stroked him to ease the discomfort but he wasn't in pain; he started to paw at the CD player and I thought, no, it couldn't be. But it was! I put Boyzone back on and, hey presto, Tex relaxed, lay his head out of the window and we both enjoyed the ride.

After that it became a regular thing. I tried other ballad type music, but only that song would relax Tex. So, yes, dogs do enjoy music and are capable of having a preference.

Tex's picture adorns my shop and is on the main shop sign. I also have blown-up pictures of him in the shop and did so at the old shop, too.

After the rape there was only one place I really felt safe in the old shop and that was in the basement. A cold, dark, damp place. I would wake, if I could manage to sleep at all, and go down to that basement. Duncan later explained to me that I felt safe there as it was the only room in the building that the monster hadn't been in. Sometimes I would take one of Tex's pictures with me and stare at it. I would longingly stare at him, missing my guardian, and sometimes I would get really angry with Tex, with the picture, or both.

I was angry with Tex, because if he had have been alive then the monster would not have raped me in the first place. I don't blame Tex any more.

≈ 5 ≈

Therapy

Woke up today feeling good. I'm really looking forward to dinner at Mo and Amjad's tonight. Went to Sainsbury's for some bits and pieces. Indie is becoming really good on the harness and I can trust her to wait patiently outside the store while I do the shopping. I got some wine for dinner and some of Mo's favourite goodies. Got to Mo's at eight pm, he ordered in Indian, and the three of us shared everything. My God, he looks good. The circulation body suit seems to be doing the trick.

I had tried for ages to get hold of a copy of the Torch song, *"Trilogy"*. I'd wanted Mo to see that film for years and I'd finally got hold of a copy. We watched it together and laughed at the similarities it had to our lives and our relationship. Mo and I were to fall out over something daft a few months later and, although I still stay in touch, I think we have drifted apart as "father" and "son". We both know, however, that if we need each other, we will be there. No matter what!

When I got home that night, I decided to have a look for some photos I had somewhere in the kitchen. A few years previously, when I lived in Dublin, all my photos had been destroyed in a fire. I was moving into my new home in Lucan, County Dublin, and had packed the sentimental things into the car; that included every photograph I had accrued over the years. Before the final load was moved from Mum and Dad's to mine, I thought I'd have a coffee with them before I brought the last of my "precious cargo" to the new house. I parked outside the house on Dolphin Road and thought, shit, no cigs. I walked to the local garage just at the top of the road and stopped in my tracks when I heard a loud explosion. I turned round and there it was, my beautiful yellow Renault Megane was in flames.

I ran back like the wind but Mum, Dad, Michelle and Natasha had got there before me. Rather than call the fire brigade, they were passing a saucepan of water from the kitchen tap in a conveyer belt style to each other and finally to Dad, who was throwing the pan of water onto an already burned-out car. It was like a scene from *Little House On The Prairie* when the barn would catch fire.

"I'm phoning the fire brigade," I shouted.

But Dad said I couldn't. "They'll get the Gardai involved and we don't want that, do we?"

"Yes, I fucking do," I firmly stated. And I called the brigade, who swiftly reduced the flames to a stinking metal mess.

The Gardai came and I told them it must have been kids. I have my own suspicions who burnt out my car, but shall keep them private at this point.

Anyway, I looked for the remaining photos in the kitchen and found a plastic bag tucked away at the back of one of the kitchen cupboards. I couldn't believe what I found in that bag.

In 2007 our family friend, Brenda, and her two beautiful children were murdered in their own home in Fallowfield. It was one of the largest manhunts this country has seen and a mass funeral I never want to experience again. It was also a breakthrough case in respect of forensic science. That monster was caught and received three life sentences, thank God.

I thought I'd lost the memorial card, but there it was. I stared long and hard at that card for ages, and considered the fragility of life in general. I also cried, again, for the passing of such beautiful people – Brenda, 10th February 1971-12th July 2007, a hard-working nurse at the MRI, and her two talented and beloved children; Christine, 30th October 1988-12th July 2007, and Frankie, 19th July 1993-12th July 2007.

I started to read the verse on the back of the card and realised I know it off by heart. It reads, "Our memories are our keepsakes, to which we'll never part, God has you in his keeping, we have you in our hearts." I remind myself of that verse every now and then.

I found another photo in the bundle. It was a photo of Wayne, Nathan and some other guy, on a night out in some club or other. It could have been Wayne's twenty-first, in the Tara Club in Dublin. Wayne looks happy in that photo.

I stared at it for what seems like hours, wondering how our lives have changed so much in a relatively short time. I slept that night with that photo next to me. I miss my brother so much it actually hurts.

The following day

I'm off to St Mary's today, not for counselling or anything like that, but to sign some forms for criminal injuries compensation. This government is paying me compensation for being raped.

The monster's first defence in court was that I was lying in order to get compensation. I realised this at a very early stage in the proceedings. Thing is, I was never made aware of the compensation I was to later receive, until the actual court case began. When my barrister dismissed that defence, after much mitigation, the monster tried other defences – it was rough sex bordering on S&M; it was consensual sex, we were in a relationship. That monster, like all others who find themselves in a court of law, will and do try every possible defence or denial rather than be found guilty, not because they see life behind bars as a great deterrent but because I believe they cannot and must not accept that society shall see them for what they are, sex offenders.

I took my usual route to St Mary's. A walk to Bowker Vale Tram, off at Victoria, past the minicabs, then the black cabs. (I often wondered if the black cab drivers recognised me in my court outfit of dressed in black with a bright pink scarf and long blond hair.) Up Market Street to either catch the bus to Oxford Road, or to walk three or four miles.

I decided on this occasion to walk, as I had plenty of time. I was to meet Gail in the cafe on the hospital grounds. She knew I didn't like St Mary's actual centre and especially that long dark corridor. I ordered coffee for both of us and Gail, as ever, was a little late.

We sat outside. I remember it being windy and some table umbrellas blowing all over the place but Gail, like me, was a smoker and we would risk the wind to enjoy our cigs as we chatted. When Gail handed me the green paperwork – the application for compensation – my stomach churned. How can this compensate me for almost ruining my life?

Gail explained that most, if not all, of her clients had the same reaction. She also said, in the very pragmatic way Gail speaks, that I was bloody well having that money, no matter what. I signed the paperwork and we chatted about all sorts of things.

Before I left for the journey home, via the Arndale Market to get Indie her chicken frames, I asked Gail, "How much do they pay victims of rape?" She said it depends on each case and that it would probably be five to six thousand pounds. Actually, a few weeks later I received £11,375.

The £11,000 was standard for a single rape and the £375 was for my physical injuries; not the cuts and bruises to my face and body, or indeed for the trauma cyst on my face that would later require plastic surgery, but for the mutilation of my genitalia. This made me really angry and I called the Criminal Injuries Compensation Authority (CICA) for an explanation.

The guy on the phone was very pleasant and I think was used to speaking to victims of rape, or maybe he'd had some "in house" training. I asked him why on the forms it said basically, Rape=£11,000; Injuries to Torso=£375.

He explained that their computer system did not have an option for testicles and the nearest they could come up with was torso.

This made me even more angry. Did men not get raped? Or were most men not brave or stupid enough to report it in the first place?

Months later, I was to join the Survivors Manchester editorial team. We are currently working on a hard-hitting, self-help brochure for male survivors of childhood sexual abuse and adult rape, with funding we have received from the Health Lottery and Zurich Insurance.

I was asked to write about "my experience of CICA", "What is male rape?", "My Story", "An episode of PTSD", and "Reporting Rape".

Here are my contributions to the self-help guide...

CICA – my experience

Eighteen months after being violently raped, I received £11,375 compensation from the Criminal Injuries Compensation Authority. I never asked for it or wanted it, but I signed the paperwork at some point. The £11k was the standard rate for a single rape and applies to adults and children alike, and the £375 was for my physical injuries. The rapist tried to mutilate my genitals with his teeth. The CICA forms stated £375 for injuries to my "torso". When I questioned this, they said their computer system did not give them an option for "testicles". I still wonder now, does that same computer system have an option for "vagina"?

Male Rape – Part 1, contribution to the self-help guide

What is male rape? Rape of any other human being is, second to murder, the most serious violation of that victim's human rights. For the period of the attack, it is a breach of all their rights and abuses, every aspect of that person. That abuse includes emotional, physical, sexual, personal, psychological, physiological and spiritual. I believe that regardless of the long term impact on the individual, which varies from one person to the other, Rape is Rape, whether man, woman, child, gay, straight, bisexual or transgender. Rape is rape, FULL STOP.

My Story – Self-help Guide

On 25th August, 2010 at 6.31am, I was raped by a 20-year-old man. He beat me, strangled me and threw me against the walls of my bedroom. My body froze in terror as this was happening, and whilst he raped me. I eventually found the strength to kick him off, as he sunk his teeth into my genitals.

I was covered in blood and ran from this living nightmare as fast as I could. I found the strength to call the police and to report this monster. I waited nearly a year to see him brought to justice. The case was long and complicated and very, very painful in its own right but the jury and Judge saw this man for what he is – a monster – and he was sent to jail.

My physical injuries got better and the scars eventually healed. I had plastic surgery on my face, and on the outside I would appear as normal as the next man. However, the rape has left me with Post Traumatic Stress Disorder, which I have learned to live with. It has affected my trust in people and my relationships with people. My character and personality have changed.

I have learned a lot about myself through the therapy I received, and I have made many new friends who have had similar experiences. I have also gained a new respect for life, especially my own, and I say to myself every day, "What doesn't kill you, makes you stronger."

PTSD episode for the self-help guide

It's Saturday, 24th August. The riots have started, first in London then in Manchester, and – according to Sky News – all over the country. I've closed early, as have all the shops on the row, and I can feel a really bad episode of PTSD coming on.

Key 103 news said the riots could come to Blackley. It's now 6pm and I am in full PTSD mode. Indie and I are preparing for this. I've made a bed under my bed with a quilt, and we have everything we need to get through this nightmare.

Wine o'clock has come early, too early. I'll open the Chianti later. I have a hammer at the flat door and a 12 inch bread knife beside me. Indie keeps looking at her reflection in the blade. I know the monster is locked up, but what if the prisons riot too and he escapes? I'll try to eat some of the goodies I bought earlier.

11pm, just woke up. Indie needs to go out. Just vomited all over the quilt and my heart is racing. It's the adrenalin again; my hands are numb and I'm trying to breathe. I can't call an ambulance this time, they're all too busy with the riots. The diarrhoea hasn't come this time.

Indie's been out, I've raced up the stairs and I've ventured into the lounge. Sky News is on, as ever, and the riots have got worse; mindless looting and violence. Been sick again, mainly red wine and peanuts. Going to try to sleep.

It's 4am, my stomach isn't churning as bad. The feelings in my hands have come back, almost, and my breathing is nearly back to normal. There is, however, that small matter of that moth – that tiny moth that has become, to me and Indie, a jet fighter that has dive bombed me for the past however many hours.

Going to the loo now. At least I can walk a bit more normally. Here goes.

No vomiting or whatever. Need to sleep now. That poxy moth again! I've done it, splatted the moth. I can breathe now and maybe get some sleep.

Danny later drew a picture of my episode of PTSD, again for the self-help guide...

Reporting Rape

When I first reported the monster, it was for theft and not rape. I'm not sure even now why that was, but I suppose it must have been because of fear. Fear of the unknown. What would happen, would it get to court or, most importantly for me, would I be believed?

The day after I reported the theft, I called the police and told them I needed to report him for rape. I was angry, afraid, and confused. Was it actually rape? I didn't know if the police or judicial system had technicalities in place as to what actually constituted the rape of a man.

When I did report rape, I wasn't sure who would come from the police. As it happened, it was a specially trained male detective who came in plain clothes and, importantly to me at the time, he came on his own.

He was sensitive and kind and he never questioned whether I was telling the truth or not. He believed me from the moment we met. That officer supported me through every stage of the process and, indeed, was a great support to me in court.

I also received huge support from St Mary's Centre at the Manchester Royal Infirmary. They offered counselling and, most importantly, provided me with my Independent Sexual Violence Advisor, or ISVA. She was a huge support at every stage of the procedure and supported me through the court case, and still supports me.

To me, the greatest help I received was from Survivors Manchester, and I am still involved with Survivors on a professional and social level.

When CICA finally put the money into my account, it was really strange, because that week I was under huge financial pressure to cover both the rent on the shop and the flat and also to find an extra 350 Euro for my contribution to the second round of payments for Wayne's legal fees.

I found it really weird and uncomfortable that the £375 equated to 350 Euro. Had the damage to my genitals equated in real money terms to possibly an hour's work from a Spanish solicitor? That was actually the reality.

I decided to put the money to good use and, for once in my life, I would have a car; a nice car, not an old one. I called round some of the garages and found one in Warrington which came recommended.

Lee and I finished work early one Thursday and got a cab to the garage. The salesman gave me three options for cars that I could drive away with there and then. One was a new Renault Megane. It was pink and looked like a frog from behind, but it was – the man said – "highly economical". The second option was an Astra, gold in colour but slightly older than the Megane. Lee said he'd rather walk home than be seen in either of those.

The only option was the third – a stunningly beautiful 2008 Peugeot 207 Sport, top-of-the-range rally car, with all the extras including Tiptronic gearbox, and in my favourite car colour, silver. There really was no decision to be made, and off we drove – or fled rather – down the M62, in my pride and joy.

The car was registered in Northern Ireland and as such had an NI number plate VLZ XXXX. I joked to Lee that I would tell people it was a private reg. But what could it stand for? Lee questioned out loud.

After a long silence Lee said, "I've got it."

"What?" I asked.

Lee pointed at my head and said, "Very large zit."

We laughed and joked as we always do, all the way home. Of course, when we got to Lee's he told Big Steve, his stepdad, and his mum, Michelle, that HE had chosen the car. Secretly, I knew he was right, as I'd quite fancied myself in the pink Megane.

≈ 6 ≈

Victim Impact Statement

A Tuesday, some time later

Woke early today, got a very full day ahead. Mo's just text: "Have you had your HIV results yet?"

I rang him and told him not to worry, I'd had the results last Friday but forgot – no, chose – not to tell anyone.

You see I'd been here before. Six months before the rape, I had kicked my ex, Matthew, out of my home and my life. Matthew was a civil servant working at a Jobcentre.

We met in 1993 and had slept with each other a few times over the years, but then we met again on one of my trips to Manchester whilst living in Dublin. I fell in love with him all over again and he's the reason I moved back to Manchester and set up the first Park Dog Grooming Salon in Prestwich.

Matt was a little older than me, and quiet, but could party with the best of them. Looking back, I think the biggest and best part of our relationship was the sexual part.

To put it bluntly, he'd try anything and as often as he could. We'd both been tested for STDs at the beginning of the relationship, but Matthew held a deep dark secret. He was HIV positive, but forgot to mention this to me.

When I found out, I kicked him out and have only seen him twice since. I went immediately for an HIV test and, by some miracle, it was negative. However, I had to wait three months for the second test and again, by some miracle, it was negative.

I swore from that day that I would not have unprotected sex again. I didn't, but obviously the last thing a rapist thinks of when raping someone is "have you got a condom?" So you see, I was quite used to living with the potential for being HIV positive and before the second three months had passed, I had already decided that I was, just to soften the blow if the result came back positive. It didn't. I had escaped this terrible disease a second time.

The positive side to this is that I have learned a great deal about sexual health and STDs in general, and I aim to stay healthy in that respect anyway.

I'm upstairs in the flat, watching Eamonn Holmes on Sky News and waiting for Lee to come in. Eamonn Holmes is talking about Kenneth Clarke, the imperfect prison system in England, and the potential for cameras to be present in court filming judges passing sentences.

I'm thinking, would I have wanted my court case to be televised? Would it have made a difference? It would to the judge, I suppose.

Would they have filmed the monster in his glass cage? Gail said on the first day in court, when I asked what he was doing when the case was being heard, that he just hung his head in shame. Was it "shame"? I wondered at the time. Or was he just acting? He was an actor after all, or so he said. He even went as far as introducing Yvonne and I to Jenny McAlpine, Fizz from Coronation Street, at the Pink Dog Show. Jenny looked more embarrassed than us.

Had she given evidence in court? Still not sure. I sent her a thank you, though, through Noirin, a neighbour of mine at the old shop. Noirin is also a Director of Corrie, and she said she would thank Jenny for me.

Some time later

Lee's not here yet. I'll have another coffee and a cig, it's only quarter to nine. Kenneth Clarke is on Sky News now. He's making a statement about cameras in court. Does he honestly believe that witnesses will turn up in court if cameras are present? The man has no clue; he's an idiot. How can he be in charge of justice? He doesn't understand the concept of justice. I'm trying not to get angry.

Lee's here; best get this show on the road, and it most certainly is a show.

It's six pm. Lee's gone home and I'm just about to leave for the group. I really hope they don't start going into the physical details of their child abuse. I can see how it helps them sharing their experiences with others who have been abused as children, but I had a great childhood and don't think I can listen to any more of that intense detail.

Back home now, it's ten pm and I need a drink. Yet again, one of the guys from the group, who's in his forties, spoke about "smell"; something that I had not ever considered before. What he said was, "I can still smell his cock."

We all helped him to get through this at the session, including me. But a very strange thing, no, a terrible thing happened on the way home. As I walked down Cross Street towards Victoria to catch the tram, all I could think or try not to think about was "smell".

When I got to the tram, the door opened and stood in front of me was a young and fashionably dressed black guy, probably on his way to or from a night out. I got on the packed tram and stood very close to him, and then it hit me. The smell of coconut oil from his neatly trimmed Afro.

Shit! That had never happened before and I didn't want it to happen again. I struggled to stay on that tram, actually getting off at a stop too early at Crumpsall. I walked the

PTSD off on the way home. I've decided not to go to the group again.

Tuesday – one week later

Had a good day today, been really busy. Lee is doing really well with the grooming. He said he could do tomorrow too, as Emma has to have the day off.

Rita popped in today too. She asked if little Charlie, her grandson, could come straight here after school and she would pick him up at 3.45. She hasn't read my angel cards for a while, but she said she'd read Lee's tarots when she gets a chance. Rita also does Reiki and has offered to heal my PTSD, if I just open my mind to it. Told her I'll stick with the angel cards.

Today is a big day, we have a royal visitor, Plumbob, my dad. Dad was over for his big brother John's wife's funeral. Anne had tragically died at 69. I'd only met Anne a few times, but she seemed really nice and will be missed greatly by Uncle John.

Lee was dead excited at the prospect of meeting Dad; he'd heard so much about him, the great tales of Dad's physical strength and his intelligence. Mainly I spoke about Dad as a man who cared deeply about his family and who would never leave any of us in times of need. And, as in any big close family, there were many times when all of us turned to Dad for help, whether that be practical or just for advice from a man who it appeared had seen and done it all.

Linda and Dad got here at 2pm and stayed for a coffee and a chat. I greeted Dad as I always do, with a big hug and a kiss. Not sure he liked the kiss bit, but I did it anyway. Maybe I did it to wind him up, or maybe I just needed a hug from my dad right now.

It's clear to me that Mum hasn't told him what happened to me. I wanted it kept that way, as I really don't think he could handle it. It would make him angry and, with his health not being too clever, anger on that level wasn't an option. Dad and Linda didn't stay long, but Dad was clearly impressed with the shop and with the ever-cheerful Lee. They left after a while and drove up the road to visit Uncle Liam and Auntie Tess.

Tuesday – a week later

Just back from the group. I decided I was being silly saying I wasn't going again. I had come to understand that just because I don't talk about the details of the rape, that didn't mean that the other guys didn't benefit by discussing their abuse. Each to his own was my motto now; as far as therapy was concerned anyway. The group was intense tonight.

Had I made someone cry? Yes, I did. And Simon told me that not only had I made him cry, I'd also inspired him to take his monster to court after more than thirty years. It would later transpire that just before his monster's trial began, he did what many of them do, he committed suicide.

An admission of guilt many people say, or the desperation of an innocent man; in Simon's case the courts will never get a chance to decide. We at the group know the truth, however. Simon's legacy of abuse has almost destroyed his life, and his monster was indeed a monster.

Duncan had talked and talked, sometimes not allowing other people NOT to talk; but that was his job, I suppose. A job he didn't even get paid for, but a job nonetheless.

Danny was fine. He had turned up. He was on one or two doses of methadone a day and not six of heroin, so yes, Danny was good. There was a new guy in the group, Gavin. He is from Northern Ireland and has long hair like mine. The theme of the group seemed to me anyway to be "historical or current". I was the only member of the group whose abuse was current; in all the other guys' cases it was historical.

As we talked, we came to a conclusion – a very important conclusion in my case, and indeed for the future of the services who assist victims of such crimes. That conclusion was that the sooner a person got help from whatever services they choose to engage with, then the faster and more complete their recovery is likely to be. I got help almost immediately, unlike most, if not all, of the other guys who had kept their "dirty little secret" just that, a secret.

In many cases, the perpetrators of their abuse were dead, or the case would be considered by the police to be too historical to secure a conviction.

I enjoyed the group tonight. Another friend from the group, Tim Hotham, wrote a poem and sent it to me by email.

It reads...

Hurt? – YOU can't hurt me any more
I'm impervious to pain
Kevlar coated to the core
I could weep to think of all the years I've spent
Destroying all around AND me AND more
'Was it my fault?' 'Am I BENT?'
Well, Mr. Wolf, those days are spent.

Forgiveness – so I'm told
Will work wonders for my soul
Fuck that, I hope the fears I've felt
Have haunted you ten-fold.

No longer when you walk the street,
Are you the power, I the meat!
Each knock, each ring, the footsteps in your wake,

Will fill you with a dread so strong,
I hope you sweat and shake.
That smell of Kouros, sunbed warmed, enough to make me sick.
Does it smell good with your denture cream, you wizened, worthless prick!

I demand my life back now, you see
Without my badge of shame.
Damaged goods? No more. NOT ME!
The real Simon's back again.
Forgive you? No, can't manage that.
'Forgetness' now, that's my game.
So jog on you pathetic twat,
Unknown perv, ah, what's your name?......

That night at the group, Simon and I went for a pint afterwards in a pub next to Nobles Amusement Arcade in Piccadilly Gardens, a known haunt for rent boys and their punters; the arcade, that is, not the pub.

We discussed how he was feeling about his ever-nearing court case. I asked Simon if the police had asked him to do a Victim Impact Statement. They had but he hadn't started it yet. I told Simon of my own experience of writing my own Victim Impact Statement.

Very soon after my original video interview, Gareth asked me to write a statement about how rape had impacted on my life. At the time I remember thinking, well it's early days and we haven't even been to court. So I told Gareth I'd get round to it. There were no rules, it could be as long or as short as I wanted it to be and, most importantly, I could say what the hell I wanted.

One day, a few weeks later, Gareth called me at the new shop, which had just opened its doors to the public. He rang about something which I cannot recall right now, but right at the end of the conversation he asked if I had five minutes.

"For what?" I asked.

He said he'd take some notes if I would relay my Victim Impact Statement to him over the phone.

I could not believe it and told him in no uncertain terms that I would write it, not speak it, in my own time and he would get it when I decided. I hung up on him.

I called Duncan and Gail and complained to them about what dickhead Gareth had done, and they both told me to calm down and just ignore him. Gareth later apologised for that very big mistake.

That night, I got back to the little flat in Newton Heath and I thought I'd better make a start on the statement.

I searched the flat high and low for some A4 paper, or even a jotter of some sort. I couldn't find any and decided to go to the local shop with Indie. I got nearer to the shop and decided that I couldn't go in. There was a gang of lads outside and I wasn't brave enough to push through them, so I gave up and went back to the flat.

I started dinner and, when fetching a knife from the kitchen drawer, I thought Eureka! There was a full packet of A4 envelopes in the drawer. That night I started to write my statement and a covering letter.

It took me six months to write that statement, but I did it. I brought it to work one day as Gareth had said he would pick it up at some point. I was having a particularly bad day and as I didn't have a car, I rang Yvonne and asked her could she take me to Bury Police Station.

Yvonne came straight over and we drove on the M60 to the station. I cried all the way to the station, and to this day I don't know why. Poor Yvonne, I'm not sure what she made of it all but hey, it's in the past now. When I got to the station, I asked for Gareth but he was out. The lady officer behind the counter asked could she help, so I told her I wanted to hand in my statement. She said she could take it, but looked a bit baffled when she reached into the bubble wrap A3 brown envelope and pulled out my "statement".

"I couldn't find any paper," I said quite abruptly, and I told her to take it as I needed to get out of that police station. She gave me a receipt and we left.

The following day Gareth rang and said that he couldn't understand a word of my statement as my handwriting was that incomprehensible. I told him that was his problem as I wasn't going to do it again. He said not to worry and that he would get a handwriting expert to decipher it.

Two handwriting experts later, Gareth rang to say they had managed to type it up. He would come to my shop a few days later with another senior officer to have me sign the typed version. Lee and I were in the shop when he arrived. I had been dreading it and, on cue, my PTSD kicked in big time.

I tried to suppress it but the trembling and stomach churning got worse and worse. I signed the statement, however, and the other officer said I had to read it.

"No, I don't," I said. "I trust Gareth." And indeed I did. The statement I wrote, and which was eventually placed in front of the Judge, reads...

Statements of John Lennon

4th May

*Today is the 4th May. I was at the police station in Bury yesterday. Yvonne brought me as I had to sell the car a couple of months ago. I'm going there again today **not** because I'm being asked to sign a "Medical Consent Form" but because I decided to hand in my "Victim Impact Statement". It's written on A4 envelopes but Gareth said that's OK. Work is going great, Sarah's looking after the shop and Emma is helping out. Indie's back to herself, family are fine and I should have a new flat any time in the next few weeks. I need to give Gareth the statement because my time is needed for my son. His cancer is in remission and he's moved back to Manchester but he still has a long way* *to go.* **THE MONSTER** *will* **not** *interfere with his recovery so whatever I wrote on the envelopes will just have to do. I need to get on with my life.*

John Lennon

Victim Impact Statement

I am writing this (sometime in December) because I have been asked to by the Police. This is because I refused the offer of a video-link and even the offer of screens around where I will be standing.

It took a long time for me to come to terms with being in that courtroom and involved many meetings and discussions with Gail from St Mary's, Gareth the policeman, and Duncan from Survivors Manchester

However, it took me a split second at a session with Gail, who explained my options. She talked for a long time and gave me insight into being in court after rape. I didn't hear much of what she said but then she explained about video-link. I decided instantly that I would face the monster in the eye. As I am writing this, that is the plan, and I will tell the court what he did to me.

He came into my life not invited, but not directly un-invited, because he scared me. I think he was looking to run from the mess he had made of his own young life. He probably thought I was his next source of money. His lies came thick and fast and I knew he had to get out of my life. My life wasn't perfect, it wasn't even good but I was getting better. I was single then and still am. I was asked to write this to explain the impact of rape on me. Rape is different, I am told, for everyone.

You see, Jury and Judge, it is the first and last time that any person will rape me. I feel I need to explain where I was before the monster, in order to explain the impact this has had on my life and me.

After a couple of years being back in a relationship with Matthew, who I'd known for 16 yrs, I'd sold my house in Ireland to be with Mat. We were planning our wedding. He was, maybe still is, a civil servant and I'd left my life in Dublin to start a new life with him. I opened up

"The Park Dog Grooming Salon" and, although not easy, I created a great little business in Prestwich. Everything was perfect, the location being the most "important" thing. The business was new and faced a lot of competition but I was fighting fit and in love. That was then!

Matthew rang me after leaving one Tuesday morning to go to work. I knew there was something wrong but nothing could have prepared me for the truth. He had had an affair, a relationship or sex with someone behind my back. I knew because he told me in that call that he was HIV positive. I waited three months to discover that I was not.

A few weeks later, my beloved dog, Tex, died. I had to make the decision based on the quality of life he had. I had great support from family and friends. The vet made a mess of it because Tex was so big. He was big and strong and would have willingly laid his life down for me, as I for him. But the seven years' vet training meant nothing as that vet brutalised my Tex as he lay in my arms.

At one stage in my recovery, I blamed Tex for not being there to stop him. I don't blame Tex or Indie. As I'm sure you can imagine, my trust in people was at an all-time low. But I had my little business, even had a few nights out. Life was, a while later, OK again.

The monster walked into my life and everything changed. Until I made the call to the police a couple of days or so later (cannot explain that period), I have no recollection or understanding of my life then. It was full of fear and the fear took over. Was he going to come back? He came back, you see, after the rape and assault. I don't know how to separate rape from another human biting into my genitals and leaving me with the impact of not being able to go to the loo, let alone anything that involved using my penis. The monster has taken my potential for a normal life away.

I was afraid of people, that fear was heightened in that place. That place was my home, my bedroom, my bed. It was also my workplace. A very public workplace with my phone number on the eighteen foot sign for everyone to see. I have never slept in that room since.

I decided that I had to move and went through many thought processes and casualties in my private life before the ultimate decision had to be faced. I was spending time, normally at "silly o'clock", in the basement, a dark damp place – but a safe place.

Sarah and I looked for a new shop, in fact, everyone did, which we eventually found and I signed a lease. That sounds easy but it wasn't. I'm now facing a bill for somewhere between £24,000 and (I am now hoping) £3500. I will deal with that.

It's now 2:30am. Ray sent me a message, Yvonne was on the phone, Linda didn't ring (but that's OK). I went to town today, on my own! I put my "Duncan" hat on and went to town. I bought a new outfit for Linda's party. I am really proud of myself.

I should explain where I'm living. It's a flat, a council flat but it's not mine. I rent it from a friend. I have a new shop now. Sometimes I walk 12 miles to and from work. The car, the "new" car, has no insurance or tax so I can't drive it. When I can afford to get it legal I will, or maybe I'll get another car. Or maybe I'll get a flat, which I applied for with a housing association, just down the road from work. I don't know what I'll do. That's how my life has become, particularly as I knew I was drinking too much; I don't know when that was.

I'm now getting ready for another day. I've brought Indie for her walk and she hasn't tried to attack the black man, a nice man who goes to his work every morning at about 6am. She's fixed, almost; I am not. That man has no argument with me. My fear of people has affected every aspect of my life. I get angry when the radio or the news reports rape. I get angry when people, my own family, use the word rape. I get angry and that anger is not part of my personality. I'm angry with the monster.

I'm drinking coffee now. Indie is in season, work is good. I can walk through the streets some days with my hat, which hides my face, on – and some days I need it. I'm going to work when the taxi gets here, with Indie. No doubt Gareth will call about the phone, my mobile, my old mobile. I dread that call. It's daft really, but the people helping me are the people I don't want talk to. It's just another day and a day I want to get through without any reminders of the monster.

I'm wearing my hat today!

Feb 3 2011

I need to explain my road to recovery as this has impacted on my life, because, you see, the people I didn't want in my life became the most important people in my life. These were the people who I realise now were helping me out. Police, doctors, nurses, Gail and Duncan.

You see, they gave me the ability to say the word rape. At some stage I became very, very, very aware that rape was everywhere. Abuse, power was everywhere. Every newspaper, every radio, TV and what, to me, became every conversation. Sarah was afraid to mention Emmerdale. I had a go at my sister Linda, for not STOPPING my beloved brother-in-law, Malley, saying that word. My own mother, my dearest, most beautiful, kindest and most thoughtful mum, had said it. She didn't mean it. But then she realised by a tone in her voice that she'd said it, but she didn't need to apologise; she's my mum.

There was a day in work, I had one of my wobblies (that's my term for when I have to remind myself that it's not happening again, dust myself down and get on with my day). Sarah – wonderful and mature beyond her years, Sarah (she reminds me of Mum) – and I were bathing a dog when another rape or abuse case (it may have been the case of the girl found Christmas Day – Jackie, I think she was called) was on Key103. I was so fed up that day I think I may have frightened Sarah as I nearly punched the radio but got on with my day. I'm sorry, Sarah, and writing this I don't even know if you will hear that apology. That day Sarah booked a dog in, a greyhound bitch. She handled the consultation. Fay was working (Fay was our Saturday girl, still is when we need a hand and can afford the £20 we give her).

Sarah told me in passing that the dog had been abused. The owner had told her, as Sarah understands. We listen to the 'abuse' of dogs all day and normally the 'rescue' involves going to the dogs' home and spending £70 to £110 on a dog. If Sarah is listening to this right now, then smile at the very least. I don't expect a laugh right now.

The dog caught my attention, as he had been abused. I wanted the owner to realise that that dog needed extra help to be a bit more treated like a dog and not a substitute child. I hadn't asked the dog's name.

Sarah told me his name was quite extraordinarily, "Ripper". I tried to use a look of disgust and eventually confronted the owner to ask him why he'd called a dog "Ripper". I didn't hear his explanation.

I was watching Sarah and him (the owner). Fay and Sarah held this terrified dog down to clip his nails as they needed doing. All I could hear was "Ripper", "Ripper", "Ripper". I was so upset with Sarah, disappointed, then I realised she didn't understand the word. The new word is rapist. I wonder when the day will come that a collie or mastiff called rapist will walk through the door?

End.

≈ 7 ≈

Unlikely Friendships

Simon had said he would start his own Victim Impact Statement that very evening, but it wasn't needed after all.

Later on in our friendship, Simon came to Manchester Crown Court with me. It was Monday, opening arguments, swearing in of the Jury and other legal requirements. I was there for Kelly (name changed for protection). Somehow this 15-year-old angel had come into my life. Her mum, Jackie, and I are now good friends.

During the lunch break, Simon sat on the steps outside the court whilst I paced up and down, smoking cig after cig. We were both angry; angry with the filth we had listened to, the unimaginable abuse that young girl had endured at the hands of a man she trusted – a man, no monster, that she had seen as her father for nearly 10 years. Simon was avidly texting.

"What are you doing, Simon?" I asked.

"I'm writing a poem," he replied. "I'll text it to you."

That poem was full of anger, and months later I would change it with help from many others. That poem is now the basis of a song, a beautiful song which would be sung by my niece, Rechelle.

After many weeks of working on it, I realised that it had no name. I wanted to call it "monster" but Lee said Rihanna would sue us.

Then, out of the blue at work one morning, Lee said, "You're a dickhead, you know."

"Why?" I asked.

"It's bleeding obvious what the song is called."

"What's that then, clever arse?"

He proudly said, "No Means No."

The lyrics of our song read...

Oh, how beautiful we are.
We know and care,
They'll stop and stare,
But they won't know.
They don't know
The pain we've all been through.
Mmm Mmmm Mmm

(chorus)
We are stronger, you'll see,
Cos the monsters agree.
The ones with the power have just won the hour.
We've taken back all the things that we lacked and we rise again with our goodness intact.
We will rise and begin
The life we live in,
Solid and strong,
No longer the wrong.
Bigger and better
And never refused.
The children are adults, are those who've been abused?

(chorus)
We are stronger you'll see,

Cos the monsters agree.
The ones with the power have just won the hour.
We've taken back all the things that we lacked and we rise
again with our goodness intact.

So I pray to all gods
That you may find the truth.
You're all better for knowing
You've not lost your youth.
We can sing once again
And will do so out loud,
you see.

(chorus)
We are stronger you'll see,
Cos the monsters agree.
The ones with the power have just won the hour.
We've taken back all the things that we lacked and we rise
again with our goodness intact.

The heavens await
All of us, cos we're great.
No-one is stronger
And no, we won't wait.
We're here and we'll sing.
Say it once out loud,
A survivor is someone who is so strong.
You'll see.

"No Means No" nearly featured in a BBC3 documentary
about life in North Manchester. They filmed us a few times,
but seemed to want to concentrate on me rather than the
song. I was never comfortable with this.

It became clear to the BBC also that I, and two other
ladies, were featuring in a BBC1 documentary "Raped", to be

screened in April or May 2013, depending on the ladies' court cases and their outcome.

I pulled out of the BBC3 programme and decided that "No Means No" would be a project for me, Rechelle, Lee and his friend, Theo, who is a wiz on producing computer-generated music.

Gail had rung me one morning and said that the BBC had commissioned two ladies to create a "fly on the wall" type reality programme about St Mary's. I wasn't sure whether or not to take part, but said I'd go along to the centre to meet Sarah and Blue, yes Blue. When I told her I thought I had a strange name but hers was even stranger, she told me she'd changed it by deed poll to Blue. Even stranger still, I thought.

One Monday morning I drove to the new St Mary's centre. I hadn't seen it yet but it was much, much better than the old centre. Gail showed me around the examination rooms, waiting area, counselling rooms, etc. and the one thing that struck me most – apart from not having a long, dark corridor – was the bright and cheerful, IKEA-style furnishings and decoration.

"Much better," I said to Gail. I waited in a small counselling room while she went to get coffee.

In they came, Gail with the coffee and Blue and Sarah with their camera, microphone and sound packs. The idea was that Gail and I would just chat about my experience of court and the centre.

Blue and Sarah introduced themselves and asked would I have any issue with not retaining my anonymity when the programme finally aired. I made it very clear that I had no issue with this, as my days of feeling ashamed were very much in the past. I explained that I couldn't understand why victims of rape went on various TV shows to discuss their ordeals and yet, for some reason, they had their faces and voices disguised.

"No!" I said very clearly. "I am not ashamed of what he did to me."

With that, Blue put the sound pack on me and another on Gail. They started the camera and off we went. Gail and I chatted for about two-and-a-half hours. I have only included a small part of the transcript here. It concentrates predominantly on the help I received from Gail during the trial, and I hope gives the reader an insight into the victim's perspective during a high profile rape case. It reads...

JOHN LENNON INTERVIEW TRANSCRIPT, 19th March, 2012 (in conversation with St Mary's Independent Sexual Violence Advisor, Gail Morgan).

John: I was in the witness box, trying to explain the burn mark on my arm and, because the Judge was partially deaf, I kept saying, "Burn, burn, burn." And he was going, "What's he saying? You what?"

Do you remember, Gail? And I got up and said, "For fuck's sake." I said, "Burn mark! There you go." But, of course, when I got up, all the ushers came running, do you remember? They slammed me down so I couldn't see him. Why would I want to see him? But there was a few funny things happened in court, wasn't there? At least on the way into court. And er..

Going to court itself.. this is what I was saying earlier.. what I expected was for me and Gail.. I wanted us to go into that court room to slay a dragon basically.. to walk in there as confident as anything and as strong as anything.. and I expected to go straight in that Monday morning and to give my evidence, to be cross-examined maybe in the afternoon.. there was even talk about that at the time.. in my head anyway.

And erm.. it didn't happen like that, cos it's nothing like that. I don't know how long it took for me to actually get to the courtroom door.. however long it took it seemed like an eternity, it seemed like a lifetime, and every time I'd get there something else would happen. I don't know why, because I wasn't in the courtroom, but something of a legal nature, arguments, legal arguments, opening arguments and closing arguments..

whatever the hell they were talking about.. erm.. I'd finally get to the door and on some occasions I'd be crawling on my hands and knees just to get to that door, literally crawling on my hands and knees with Mel and whoever else was available.

It was generally Mel holding my hand, hugging me, seeing me through as best she could to get to that courtroom door. The amount of times I just wanted to say.. Enough! I am the victim here, not the accused. But, of course, if I'd have done that and walked away, which I could have done, maybe he would have been released and found not guilty.. I don't know.. No, in fact, I think I do know.. I think I know I needed to be in that courtroom.. I wanted the jury to see.. and even looked, though I tried to look my best.. but I was a mess.. and in my heart and soul I know I wanted them to see that.. to see the level of anxiety, to see that I couldn't even walk. When I came into the courtroom, it was through a different door to everybody else.. I actually walked.. I thought he was down in "holding cells"?

Gail: *He would have been outside because he was on bail. They bring you in first and get you settled in the witness box behind the screens and then bring him in, so he wouldn't see that. And in some ways that's good.. because I think how difficult it is to.. to go to court and give evidence, that's the one thing. We talk about power and control with rape and sexual assault, and that's the one thing you don't want that person to see.. is that.. he heard you were already in that.. in that witness box.. you were there ready to give evidence. He didn't see what happened prior to you getting in that witness box, which for me.. and it isn't about me.. is a good thing, because you know.. that power and control shift is.. although it was difficult for you to do that.. the fact that you'd gone to court, you know.. you'd had that four days.. because you didn't start till the Friday*

John: *Was it the Friday?*

Gail: *It was the Friday and then you had the weekend, because you had to come back on Monday.. so all of that time leading up to that, he knew you was there ready to give your evidence, so some of that control* *shifts. You were in control, although it was difficult for you to get into that witness box and everything that surrounded that, he knew nothing of the intensity and you know what was going on in the Witness Service, because you did talk about not wanting to do it, which is natural.*

John: *It is.*

Gail: *And so, I think it's good that they don't see that, because at that point you're there ready to give your evidence and he didn't see..*

John: *The mess that I was..*

Gail: *The mess that you were.. (John laughs) no, the mess that I was.*

John: *It's true.*

Gail: *And that works.. pros and cons.. that works for the jury to see the difficulty someone has giving evidence, because I think what happened with yourself was that you wanted to go into that courtroom even though it was with screens. You wanted to go into that courtroom, you didn't want to do it via video link, you wanted to be in there, and that's why your video was transcribed into a statement, so that you could go into court. Because again, it's about that control.. ok, you're behind a screen but he knows you're there.. you know.. it's not.. Sometimes it's far removed if you're doing it via a video link and the jury don't see that emotion. There might have been emotion in your video, but it's very different seeing that sort of head and shoulders.. because I think you can become slightly more relaxed once you get used to that video, because the only person you're seeing are the people that are asking you the questions.. Whereas you've talked about.. you know, those eyes of the 12 members of the jury on you.*

John: *And they were, and they were.*

Gail: *And so, yeah, it was extremely difficult for you but..*

John: *Hardest thing I've ever done, ever.*

Gail: *But you did it.*

John: *I did it, yeah.*

Gail: *And that's what we talked about, isn't it? Is that you have to do that.. sometimes people have to do that, regardless of whatever the outcome is because.. you know you can never, ever say how a jury is going to find.. But it is about that going in there and doing it.. and you did it! And it was very, very difficult for you.*

John: *I refused the video link right from the beginning.. and er.. I even refused the screens, if you remember..*

Gail: *You did at first.*

John: *I changed my mind and em..*

Gail: *I think it's important to say that.. you know.. special measures have to be applied for and you know.. a screen is a screen.. if on that morning you'd have felt, I don't want the screens, the screens wouldn't have been in place, but if you'd have said right from the word go, no, I definitely don't want screens and then on the morning of the trial decide I want screens that would have then delayed it even further, because they then have to be applied for. So it's easier to say, Well, we'll get the screens in place; if you want them, they're there, if you don't, they can be taken away.*

John: *I'm glad I had the screens.*

Gail: *Yeah.*

John: *Now I'm glad I had the screen. Initially I think I was like slaying the monster-type thing, and I'll see him in court, and I'll tell them this and I'll tell them what happened, and the whole lot erm.. but when it came to it, I don't think my evidence would have been as clear.. as erm..*

as strong.. as.. if I'd have been able to see him. Cos I think what I would have wanted to do was just turn around and go back out, or not come in at all, you know, looking back.

John: *We had what's called a.. Gail came with me.. something that St Mary's do.. I don't think I could have accessed it without St Mary's to be honest.. a pre-court visit.*

Gail: *You can, the Witness Care can do that but often it's.. you know I tend to.. any, any clients of mine that I'm dealing with going to court, I will always.. I think it's important to go on that pre-court even if you're having it via video link.. and I would go with you to that pre-court visit.*

John: *And it was important and we went..*

Gail: *We went..*

John: *Me and Yvonne, wasn't it?*

Gail: *It was.*

John: *And we got to go through.. and what I wasn't expecting and see, if I hadn't have done the pre-court visit, there are certain things I saw in a court .. such as being in the barristers' chambers.*

Gail: *That's very unusual, that's very unusual.. because Bolton Crown Court is such a small court.*

John: *I thought it was huge.*

Gail: *No, it's not. It's such a small court.. where the Witness Service is situated.*
John: *You have to go through, don't you?*

Gail: You have to go through the barristers' room to go out the side, cos there's always a separate entrance. That is very unusual because in the other courts, in Manchester and Liverpool, that doesn't happen.

John: There's none of that.

Gail: You see. It is such a small court. So it's quite amusing really.

John: It is, yeah.

Gail: You have to knock, because they could be talking about the case and you have to go through and then you have to knock back.

John: And his barrister as well.. whatever.. his barrister was in that room actually during the court case. And, of course, I couldn't.. I just wanted to be polite and if I'd looked and said, Hi, or Good morning, he'd just turn away like that and would completely ignore me. And I couldn't get my head round this, you know, being a polite person, being a friendly person. But no, we had to walk through this room.. and I'm so glad we went on the pre-court visit because Sue, who facilitated with us or whatever, she started off with the small courtroom, do you remember?

Gail: That's right.

John: And we built our way, worked our way up to the actual courtroom, which was enormous, do you remember? It was huge. To me it was a football pitch, it was absolutely enormous. And I was kind of like nonchalant about it and whatever. And Sue said, have you been in court before? And I said, for silly little things, driving offences whatever, but never actually been to a proper big court, Crown Court. And she brought us into the smaller one, do you remember? Did we see three?

Gail: No, two, there's a smaller court and then that one.

John: *And then the big one that I was in. We went into the smaller one and I even got to sit in the witness box and do the swearing, you know, and all this and hold my hands on the Bible or whatever it was. And it was quite amusing really, you know, we were pretending me and Yvonne and yourself even, do you remember, to be in court and all that? Then, when she showed me the door that I would have to walk through the actual courtroom that I was in, and she said, "Are you ready for this?" And I was like, it's only a bloody room, isn't it? Well, then she opened it and I went, Fucking hell, and she said, "Yes, John, Fucking hell." It was just huge and I really wasn't expecting it. And it kind of reminds you of how small you actually are in the scheme of things, that's how you feel and think, how can I go into this bloody courtroom? And the public gallery was quite a big area. I'm thinking, now hang on.. and you don't even know at that stage if there are going to be people in the public gallery. And I kept maintaining all along, still do, why would anybody in their right mind – and you're gonna correct me on this, cos I've been to one recently – why would anybody in their right mind go to watch a rape trial in a public gallery? But actually, I've done that recently for a young friend of mine who asked me to be there, and that wasn't so good either but we got through it. And he got 11 years, so that was good.. that was a result. Yeah, where am I up to? I don't even know what I'm talking about.*

The first person I told.. I suppose I'll start from there.. after not a long period.. yeah, I did think about not reporting it and I just reported the theft and I've explained all that.

I suppose I really don't fully understand why men don't report rape. I don't really fully understand that. I'm a man who's reported it. I wasn't going to report it because I thought I could deal with it. But, like everything in life that.. if you've never experienced something, you're not going to deal with it. It's your first bereavement, for example, somebody close; if that's never happened before, you think, Oh well, your world's ended because Mum's died, or somebody's died, or whatever it is. When something as.. I don't want to use the word unusual.. as horrific as rape happens to me as a man, I suppose looking back, if I hadn't reported it he may have come back. Cos he did come back. He came back a couple of times. So really that's probably why I reported it, so he wouldn't rape me again. Or he wouldn't gang rape me again with other people when he came back to the shop with other people. Fear, I think, prompted me to report it. Fear that I couldn't exist as a person, I couldn't go outside my door, certainly not run a business. And I nearly lost my business, very, very close I came to losing that business, the business I walked away from, erm, because of course the flat was above, that's where it happened. And I couldn't be in that building, I just couldn't. Erm, the point about men not reporting rape, I suppose there's the macho thing.

There's the male ego, there's the male as the provider, the protector, all the perceptions people have of men, gay or straight, or whatever, bisexual, whatever the hell their sexuality is, it doesn't really matter.

I think there's a lot of shame associated with rape and stigma that should not be associated with rape. The person who chooses to rape you chooses to do that. You don't invite it, you don't ask them to do that. As a man, I suppose men like to be physically strong, probably more so than women. As a man, I suppose I am physically strong, as a dog groomer it keeps me fit, and the whole lot of it. You're lifting dogs all day long, big ones, small ones, the whole lot of it. I suppose that's challenged that strength as a man and, er, really though, I'm very proud of myself and I know how strong I am, because he's in prison. I went through all that process that got him to prison. I know how strong I am, whether that be emotional strength, or physical strength, or both; it doesn't really matter. I suppose it is a bit of both really.

But really I'd implore any man, whatever shape, size, or whatever, to report rape or sexual assault of whatever nature. Age is something to do with it as well in my case. I was 40 and he was 20. So I suppose, as the mature man, the businessman, you're expected to have all the answers, you're expected to be the provider, the protector of everyone in my world. You know if anyone's got a few problems, they all come to John and the whole lot of it. And, er, and you help where you can. Erm, age I suppose, maybe I thought to myself, well how did I let this happen? I should have known better, why didn't I just tell him to go initially, why didn't I just kick him out?

Again, it's down to fear I suppose, erm, the fear of the unknown, the fear of mind that you don't know how stable it is or what he's capable of, and the whole lot of it.

Men.. it's a big thing for me.. I'm glad they sent Gareth along as a man, initially. Not so glad that the erm photographic evidence erm kind of happened haphazardly. Erm, there's lots of stuff I wasn't happy about with Gareth and you know that. I see now the difficulties he had.. huge difficulties he faced, for instance, the photographic evidence. He couldn't actually get a photographer to take pictures, even though there were two of them, forensic photographers, policewomen in my house the day that they came, the police. They could have just asked me to go to the bedroom or whatever, with Gareth even present, that didn't really bother me. And I wanted them to take photographs but they wouldn't because I'm a man and they were two women. Gareth couldn't find anyone within the Bury services police or whatever to actually come within a couple of days and take the photos.

When I went on my first hospital visit to North Manchester General to be examined, and then later for the HIV and the whole lot of it. Another round of HIV, yes, six months in total on the trot, erm, interestingly they saw me straight away. And I think I explained just a bit earlier to you, erm, for the infection in my finger from dog grooming, hairdresser's hand, erm, I went yesterday just to get a different antibiotic and again they saw me immediately in a very, very full A&E with some very, very sick people. And this time I challenged them. I asked the receptionist, why are you seeing me straight away? Why, am I special or something? But of course they see me straight away in case there's other issues going on. Maybe I'll be suicidal, which I've not been; at one point I was at the beginning, but I'm certainly not now. And little things like them seeing you straight away in the A&E, that to me is a very big thing. I'd rather wait 18 hours or whatever – maybe not 18, but a couple of hours – whatever it takes, rather than be seen as "special" and seen straight away. And, if it ever happens again that I have to go to hospital – touch wood, I won't – well, I'll be asking them to make me wait like the rest of the people, triage me as a normal person and not this person who's been raped. Because in order to move on and get on with your life and be a "survivor", you really want to erm.. do I have to use the word rape any more? Cos it happened then, it's not happening now, you know, so there we are.

Yeah, the first person I told was my mum in Ireland during the court case. Would you believe his barrister actually phoned my mother in front of me, pretending to be his solicitor and asking for information – yeah, in front of me. Cos, as I said, you had to walk through the barristers' chambers, or is chamber the right word? I think it might be. And, er, in front of me he made that phone call cos I had a text message from my sister to say my mum was on the phone to his barrister, or solicitor, whatever the term used. Yeah. And she gave him short shrift, believe me, and more or less hung up.

Gareth wasn't too impressed about that either. He had a word at some point cos that was just not right. Mum was going through enough with other stuff in her life without having to, you know, deal with that, knowing that I was in court, and I of course would be phoning her that night, telling her how I was getting on, which the first week or whatever basically meant sitting around doing nothing, twiddling our thumbs, having coffee, trying to go for a cig if somebody would go with you, you know and stuff like that.

Gail: *I think from the actual assault to actually going to court.. when did we go to court now?*

John: *It was June 27.. how the hell I remember that when I don't remember yesterday.*

Gail: *It's imprinted on your brain.. so August to June was quite quick in..*

John: *Actually getting to court.*

81

Gail: *And we didn't have any adjournments, which are unusual really. Although we had a long time in court, there wasn't an adjournment, so it was sort of fairly quick from being arrested, charged and got into trial. But I think you were talking about.. erm, I think it's important to say for others who may be wanting to make a report or thinking about making a report, there is going to be some stumbling blocks. And I think, in my experience, maybe not so much now but in my experience with males, erm, reporting rape or sexual assault, I think there's always going to be maybe a little bit of an issue with the police that might be something that, especially a male reporting rape because predominantly in society it happens to females, doesn't it? It doesn't happen to males – you know we know different here, but you know I work really closely with the police. And I have to say there were some issues, but you know I think there were issues on both sides really and I think, correct me if I'm wrong, sort of myself trying to be a mediator between yourself and Gareth because you would get frustrated if you tried to get hold of Gareth and he hadn't got back to you, erm, because obviously it's very difficult cos you're in that particular zone at that point when you need to know that information.*

John: *Well, you think in his case or in our case or my case, he's doing nothing. What's he doing? What's he doing? And then you discover kind of quickly when you get to court the amount of work that's actually gone on. Massive work, and I mean massive.. I'll give you an example.*

End

The above transcripts are only a small part of a three hour interview.

The second time Blue and Sarah filmed me was at the shop, they wanted to film me working. Emma and Lee were working with me that day, a Tuesday. They had said they didn't want to be filmed, but when the day came they both came in their good clothes and Emma even had make-up on. Lee wore a white, shiny and very expensive tracksuit and had his Armani sunglasses neatly sitting on his freshly-cut hair. Don't want to be filmed, my arse, I thought.

Blue and Sarah turned up and they started filming from the other side of the counter. I'd asked them to stay on that side as we were having trouble with an aggressive teuveron, or Belgian Shepherd.

Emma used all the Caesar Milan techniques I'd shown her and she very skilfully managed to get a lead on the dog. I walked him down towards the bath and, just as Lee and I were lifting him into the raised bath, the dog shit. Pure diarrhoea. Lee's shiny tracksuit got covered; it was everywhere.

I managed to lift the dog into the bath, but Lee screamed and hopped about, getting further covered in the shit.

"It has gone through to my fucking socks!" he shouted.

Well, we laughed that hard it was unreal. Here we were being filmed for this very serious and hard-hitting documentary, and the film crew could not even film it as they were laughing just as much as us.

When Lee finally calmed down and got most of the shit off him, he helped me to bath the dog. As we were doing just that, he said to me, "So did you have a joint last night?"

He obviously forgot I had a sound pack on, and I said to him, "Will you be fucking careful what you're saying?" as I nodded towards the mic clipped to my T-shirt.

"Oh shit, I forgot," he said.

When we got the dog into the drying cage, we all sat down for coffee and a chat. Lee asked Sarah, "Did you get all that?"

She said, "I couldn't. I was laughing too much, had to put the camera down."

"Shame," Lee said. "Could have got £250 from *You've Been Framed.*"

Blue said she'd like to film Indie and her first and only born, Jaya. His original name was Slipper, but Kelly had researched names and asked me to call him Jaya, Red Indian for victory. She was later to get victory in court.

Lee and I got into the courtesy car we'd used to get to Earl's Court for the awards ceremony. I drove the half mile up the road to my new, but very old house. We got Indie and Jaya into the car. I still had my sound pack on and it was killing Lee not to speak. He has lots of great characteristics to his personality, but not speaking was not an option in Lee's world. There was complete silence as we drove back to the shop but then, as it all became too much for him and just as we were pulling up outside the shop, he said, "I really like Blue and Sarah, but why couldn't the BBC send a couple of nice birds and not a couple of lesbians?"

My heart sank. Sarah had the sound receiver on but I still don't know if she got that or not. Nothing was ever said. I didn't see Blue or Sarah again for a while until I called them in October 2012.

He was out, the monster had finally served his full term in prison and he was now out. I had a call from Joan, from the Victim Liaison Service in Moss Side, and I made notes as she spoke on the phone. For the purposes of my book, I saved those words and named the file, "The Rapist's Words". Here are those words...

"The Rapist's words"

It's Friday, 5ᵗʰ October, 1.30pm, Joan from the Victim Liaison Service rang yesterday as I was driving up to Lee's. For a split second I didn't recognise the 0300 prefix but quickly the reality hit me. "Hi Joan."

"He's out," came the reply. I asked her to ring me in the morning. From that moment I could feel the anxiety start to creep back. As much as I tried to suppress it, the chest pains and stomach churning had started

but my mind was in perfect control, no flashbacks or feeling the need to hide away from the rest of the world. I brought Indie and the hugely impressive Jaya to bed with me that Thursday night, something I never do. I didn't sleep much but got a couple of hours, I think.

Sure enough, in work the following morning Joan rang. She opened his file on her computer which she said was running slow and gave me some details of his release. He was released yesterday and has no restrictions, curfews or conditions. She told me he is now "of no fixed abode"; something which staggered me, as he must sign on at a police station every week for several years. He is, as Joan put it, at liberty.

I asked Joan a question which has been eating away at me since he raped me. "Did he ever show any remorse?" Joan went further into his file and started to read some of the notes the Prison Service had made, but what she read to me were his words, the rapist's words.

"I am a person of limited cognitive ability. I don't think about the consequences of my actions. I steal and don't care who I hurt. I use lies to manipulate people. I am not sorry for attacking John Lennon. I won't do it again, I want to stay out of prison."

Joan advised me to ring the police, to have my phone number and address "marked" just in case he comes near me. I did just that, but deep down I know I am stronger physically and mentally than the monster. Bring it on, monster, my monster. We'll see who ends up in hospital the next time we meet – and meet again we will, I promise you that.

The day after that call, I contacted Blue and asked her to film me one last time.

"OK," she said. "Where would you like us to meet?"

She knew he had just been released and was of no fixed abode. I was determined to be filmed in public, in the Gay Village in Manchester. Blue arranged for us to meet in Via Fossa, she was in London when I called her but had called Via to get permission to film.

I woke that day, walked Jaya, and made my way into the Village. I parked the car and wondered would the three quid I put in the meter be enough.

I was early; only 10.30am and we were due to start filming at eleven, what should I do? I decided to go for a walk in the park, Sackville Park to be precise. I'd been to the Pink dog show not once since the rape, but twice, and driven by that park a million times. But still that park left me with a chilling feeling.

I was, yet again, feeling vulnerable; vulnerable to the point of wanting to forget the three pounds on the meter and just get into my car and go home. I persevered and waited in the park for Blue and Sarah. It was freezing; I walked around the park, trying not to remember the Pink dog show or anything to do with the monster. I sat on the bench a little bewildered. What had my life come to? What was I going to speak about on camera?

I'd rung Danny on my way in to the Village. At the last Editorial Team meeting for the Self Help Guide, he had read a poem out, a poem he'd written. That poem impacted on me greatly as I now felt a part of the group and not the only member who had been raped as an adult. I asked Danny to text it to me, and for the final filming of the BBC documentary I read that poem to camera.

I sat on a chair near to Churchill's on Canal Street and I read Danny's poem whilst being filmed by Blue and Sarah. I felt particularly proud, as all three of us knew the monster could walk by at any time. It reads:

A poem by Danny Wolstencroft (dan-dan-art@hotmail.com) - Sexually abused as a child by female perpetrators and a close male family member.

86

The Shield

My jacket, hood up, zipped up, locked out from the world.

Zip, don't break, don't blow open, my confidence's been hurled.

Keeps them out and away! Please don't approach, I'm still afraid.

That's the prayer that I've just prayed to me, it is my military blockade,

Keeps Them out and keeps me sane!

My jacket.. hood up, zipped up, safely into the background I fade.

It's tiring all this keeping up the fight,

Not stepping out in the night, only walking in the light.

If I have enough, choose to jump and end it all..

My jacket it will be, hood up, zipped up.. goodbye to you all.

Danny wrote and sent me another of his overwhelming poems. It reads:

Them 3

I remember a time, I'll never forget, when THEM wrestled and overpowered my usual, happy-go-lucky positive little tiny shadow.

THEM'S shadow now casts over me.

Everything I did, said and saw was dull, tainted by THEM. Happy-go-lucky had left.. for now.. enter left of stage the positive thought police.

For what seemed like forever, from that day forth, I called them, THEM THREE. I had relinquished all control.

THEM became the director of my life, THEM wrote the script and gave it to the creative director.

All artistic licence on my life had gone.

I was cast in a little known, shadowy film called "Forever Silent". Amen, I was now a B movie actor on the path to self-sabotage.

Don't actors take drugs to perform and to cope? Forever the optimist, "I'll make my time on stage comfortable and fun."

Little did I know this was all part of the script, I was following THEM'S plan.

THEM had been fervently writing, deeper into the silence I fell, fell and fell, my thoughts were not my own.

Chip, chip, chip; confidence, check; self-worth, check; belief and hope, check; check. All gone. I'd lost it! Whatever it was. Did it matter? I was gone.

Manipulated with a bag of sweets, I jumped onto the dusty mat, down the helter skelter, I went and went.

This is a long slide, I thought, then, bump!

I hit the bottom, rock bottom, or what I like to call temporary lodgings, a self-contained flat, just as THEM had written.

THEM for a time had won..

Silence reigned on THEM'S throne.

A breakdown was next, and a stutter followed, but what's this? Two arms, two legs and a head, I'd survived the fall.

Vowel by vowel I became vocal, the silence broke, I shouted.

I told what the collective THEM 3 had done.

Ahhh, lighter.

To the director's room I positively marched with strength, BANGED on the door and picked up a glass of neverending pure water, I poured it over the script until the ink diluted and ran, that's when clarity began.

Now I'm in charge "whatever it takes".

I believe I've reclaimed my own shadow, I'm sat here now re-writing the script.

This is HOW my new life began, I will achieve.

    I wouldn't see Blue or Gail again until the pre-screening of the documentary.

On the same day that Blue emailed the transcript of the interview at St Mary's, I received another email from Gareth. It was the transcript of my original video interview.

It reads:

≈ 8 ≈

My Video Interview - transcript

"*O*n *the 7th September, 2010, I attended Bury Police Station and provided a video interview in relation to an incident that happened to me on Wednesday, 25th August, 2010. At the time of that incident I owned the Dog Grooming Salon, at 399 Bury Old Road, Prestwich. This is a three floor property, the ground floor being the shop and workspace, the first being the living room and kitchen and the attic space being the bedroom.*

I first met the monster on a Saturday around four to five weeks prior to the 25th August, 2010. Myself and Sarah were working in the salon when the monster walked into the shop. It was obvious that he was gay; I am gay myself, you can just tell. He asked if he could borrow £2 to get to a village in Manchester, he said that it was his birthday and that the bank machine had swallowed his card. Up until this day I did not know the monster, I had never seen him and never spoken to him.

Maybe a week later he came back into the shop to say hello. He was very friendly, always smiling and cheerful. We talked for a bit and I quite liked him.

The monster next came to the shop on the Friday morning, this being the 20th August, 2010. A neighbour, Brian, was already at the shop, we were chatting with another local lad called Tony. We were all chatting, having a brew and cigarette at the front of the shop. The monster turned up and asked could we have a chat inside? We both went into the shop and stood next to the counter. The monster asked, could he take me for a drink? I said yes, I was flattered. I gave him my business card with my number on it, after a few minutes he left. I went back outside and told Sarah that he had just asked me out. Before leaving, he asked could he pop down tomorrow? I said yes.

The next day, Saturday the 21st August, the monster arrived at the shop at about lunchtime. Me and Sarah were working in the salon, the monster said he would watch us work and spend the day with us. Later the three of us went to Brian's to look at a new fish tank that he had bought. I invited the monster to come with us. We all got quite drunk, I was really drunk. He stayed the night in my bed with me, I couldn't remember the night. Nothing of a sexual nature happened on the Saturday night. During the course of this Saturday, he had stated to me that he worked at River Island in the Arndale Centre, Manchester. He told me that there had been a mix-up with his wages; over the next few days I discovered that monster was lying to me about working at River Island.

On the Sunday morning, whilst still in bed, myself and the monster had a kiss, a bit of a fumble; by this I mean masturbation. This was over in ten minutes. We both did it to each other until we ejaculated; I couldn't say who instigated this. We were up for about nine o'clock; we went for breakfast at Heaton Park Café and had a pleasant morning. We then went back to the shop and I groomed my dog ready to go to The Pink dog show, this was starting at 12 o'clock. Before setting off we walked the dog and then caught a taxi to the Gay Village where the dog show was. Once there, we met Yvonne, a close friend of mine, Phyllis, Geoffrey, and his partner, Andy. The monster kept introducing me to people as his boyfriend. He was holding my hand and kissing me, I thought it was all a bit too much. The monster told me that he was an actor, he introduced me to Jenny, she plays Fizz in Corrie. The girl was embarrassed as if she didn't know him. He was very over-the-top, too much too soon for me. I thought, I'm too old for all this but went along with it. After the dog show, we all went for a drink near to the canal, Geoffrey and Andy then left. Yvonne invited myself and the monster to go back to her house, Yvonne drove as she does not drink. On the way back to Yvonne's, we stopped at an off licence, the monster bought a big bottle of wine. This is when I realised that the monster had drink issues. We stayed a while at Yvonne's and then she drove me and the monster back to my address. The monster stayed the night.

The following morning he rang in work stating that he was sick. He remained at my address until later in the afternoon when he borrowed twenty pounds off me and went to meet a friend in town. The monster was back at mine by 6pm, I could tell that he had been drinking and had with him a bag of cannabis. He had some cannabis on Saturday and always seemed to have some with him. By now I was getting pissed off with him a little, I couldn't get rid of him. I said, is it not time that you went back to your flat? I even offered to drop him off. He said, "I don't want to go back, I'll go back tomorrow." I told Yvonne and Sarah that I couldn't get rid of him, he just wouldn't go. He ended up falling asleep on the couch stoned, and I went to bed. I really wanted him away from me. I was going to say to him tomorrow, you need to go.

On the Tuesday morning he told me that he had to be in work at ten o'clock to cover for someone. He told me that a girl at work had lent him £100 and that he was covering her shift because her boyfriend had just been caught cheating on her. By now I had formed the opinion that he didn't work at River Island and that he was just lying to me. In the morning I woke him up and he left. The monster came back to the shop at about two o'clock in the afternoon.

I can't be certain if the above two days were the other way about, it could be that on the Monday he went to work but said to the manager he was sick and that's why he came back early.

On the Tuesday evening, this being the 24th August, 2010, he asked could he cook me dinner before he went back to his flat? His character started to change on the Tuesday. He was in the kitchen cooking, he had the music on full blast in the living room, he had rewired the woofer with the TV. He was smoking cannabis. I went into the kitchen and knocked the cannabis onto the floor by accident. He jumped up and down and had a tantrum like a child, he was shouting and swearing. I went into the living room, after a few minutes he came in and said sorry. I asked him to turn the music down because I have neighbours. He had another paddy; he was all wound up, banging the walls. I saw a difference in him and it really scared me. It is then that I realised he had to go. I rang Yvonne from the kitchen and told her what was happening, the music was still going full blast. Yvonne said that she would come over but by the time she had arrived, the monster had turned the music off and put the TV on in the living room. He had music on from the shop, it was on just as loud. I was frightened of him now, I didn't know what he was capable of.

Yvonne stayed for tea. He had cooked a chicken dish and rice. He was smoking his cannabis; he had been heavily smoking this but he hadn't drunk that much alcohol. We had a very pleasant hour, he was telling funny stories and stuff. I told Yvonne I needed to get rid of him, she suggested that I leave it until the morning. After Yvonne had left, the monster went to bed upstairs. This was about half ten till eleven. I stayed in the living room watching TV. I'm not sure what time it was when I went upstairs, it was very late. Nothing happened in bed. I made up my mind by now, I just went to sleep. The monster had earlier tried to kiss me in the kitchen, I didn't want to encourage him so didn't kiss him back. I wanted the monster out of my life. If I had gone along with his advances it would have made things worse, I thought he would have seen me as his boyfriend.

On the Wednesday morning, this being the 25th August, 2010, I woke up early about 0545hrs and went downstairs. I woke the monster up first because I thought he had to be up for work. He had, on the Tuesday, told me that he was doing an 8am-8pm shift on the Wednesday. He said it was his punishment for not going in earlier in the week. He said, "I'm not in work till 9, why have you woke me up?" I asked him if he wanted a coffee, he said, "No, I'll have a beer." It was only about 6am. I made myself a coffee in the kitchen and then went into the living room, watching the news headlines on the TV. The monster came down and went into the bathroom and then went back upstairs. Money was on my mind, because the rates were due. I went into the kitchen and saw that around four hundred pounds was missing from the takings from the shop; this money was in a drawer in the kitchen. I assumed that the monster had stolen it. I didn't think Sarah had stolen it because I trusted her. She deals with the money from the shop all the time and never has it been missing.

I went upstairs and confronted the monster, who was now lay in the bed drinking the beer. I was scared of him and wanted him out of my life. The attic room is quite big and the bed is in the middle of the room. He was wearing an open denim shirt and a pair of socks, nothing else. I was wearing a housecoat (dressing gown). I was naked underneath this; I normally sleep naked. I said, "Monster." He replied, "What?" He was pretending to be half-asleep. I said, "There's money missing, did you take the money from me? I need to know." The monster jumped up from the bed and was shouting, "I ain't fucking taken any money." I was stood to the left hand side of the bed, he was in the middle of the bed. He stood up at the side of me and grabbed my housecoat, throwing me onto the bed. I was face down. I caught my head slightly on the end of the bed. The monster was stood up at the side of bed, he was thumping the mattress. I lay there silent; I froze. He continued shouting, "I didn't take your fucking money." I was waiting for him to punch me, but he didn't.

He started running around the bedroom, trashing the place. My room was a bit of a tip anyway. He slammed the front window, kicked some boxes, pulled a clothing rail over and threw my shoes about. I couldn't see him but I could hear and feel it as he moved about the room. The dog was growling; she was afraid. I thought the best option was to stay calm and he would then calm down. After five to ten minutes he did calm down. He came and sat on the bed, he was breathing funnily. I casually turned around as if I was just going to get up. He then lay down and cuddled up with me. He was looking at me as if to say everything was ok, he had a sympathetic look in his eyes like he was trying to apologise. I was flat on my back still on the bed. He started kissing my neck. I said, "It ain't happening, monster, it's not fucking happening." He put his hand onto my penis and tried to masturbate me. It wasn't erect. I kept repeating that it wasn't happening, stop it. He had hold of my penis and started to masturbate it harder, it was hurting, I told him to stop but he continued to masturbate me. I could feel that my penis was starting to go hard; I grabbed hold of his hand and moved it off my penis again, telling him that it was not happening. The monster then started to say, "I'm gonna fuck you, hard, till it makes you bleed."

The monster was sat up on the bed and I was still lay on my back. Even though he had grabbed my penis, I wasn't majorly concerned or particularly petrified. I didn't expect what happened next to happen. He was stroking my legs, he then pushed my legs back apart and was sat in front of me. I said, "What the fuck are you doing?" He kept saying, "I'm going to fuck you." I was now afraid. He had an erection, a very large erection, he knelt in front of me in between my legs. I didn't move because I really didn't think that he was going to do anything. He pushed my legs right back, he was very strong and forceful. He moved my right leg further back. I was saying to him, "What the fuck are you doing? Get off me." He had his hand forced on my chest, my leg was trapped behind his arm so I couldn't move. I was frightened by now. He shoved the head of his penis inside me, the pain was overwhelming, he didn't get it all in, because I was fighting and pushing him. He was on top of me as if we were having sex, it was about half his penis that was inside my bottom. It felt that this went on for a few minutes. He was raping me, I was struggling and I managed to push him off. He wasn't wearing a condom and he didn't ejaculate in me. I don't think he did. He penetrated me but not all the way at first.

I kicked out and he hit the foot of the bed where the headboard is. He jumped straight back up. He was trying again to penetrate me but I was

95

struggling and he couldn't. He was on his knees. He grabbed both my legs to twist/flip me over, as he did he bit my penis; he did this from behind or underneath, as I was twisting from my back to my front. The bite was nearly an inch from the base of the penis, to the left and he also bit my testicles. His teeth bit into my penis again and I screamed. The pain was how I would imagine if you were to get stabbed, it was a lot worse than a dog bite. I screamed, he pushed back and sat on the bed again. I jumped up from the bed, I still had my housecoat on, but it was open. I looked down and saw my penis was going red like a graze when ready to bleed. I could see the teeth marks. The monster then stood up on the bed and kicked me with severe force into the side of my abdomen. He then jumped on me and placed both hands around my neck; he was strangling me and I couldn't breathe. The pain in my groin was intense and I could feel the blood pouring down my legs. He forced his penis inside, deep inside me, and raped me again. At that moment I wanted to die. He let go of my neck with one hand and delivered a punch to my face that nearly knocked me out, all the time raping me. Indie was barking and growling and, without knowing where the strength came from, I kicked him off me and across the room. He jumped up immediately and grabbed my hair, dragging me off the bed with all his strength, and with both hands he grabbed my hair and threw me against the wall. My head cracked the plaster on the wall. I was begging for him to stop.

I lay on the floor and curled into a ball. He shouted for me to get up, he then grabbed my hair again and held my head back. I had no energy left. He shoved his penis into my mouth, telling me I would die if I bit him. He fucked my mouth for some time, slapping my face with his left hand whilst pulling my hair with his right hand. I was gagging all the time he was doing this. He ejaculated in my mouth and threw me onto the floor. He then grabbed my hair again, lifting my head slowly upwards. He wiped his semen all over my face and slammed my head into the wall again, I felt semi-conscious as he threw me to the floor again. I lay curled up in a ball, starting to feel consciousness leaving me. For a moment there was silence, then I heard Indie whimpering, I couldn't open my eyes but I could hear Indie. Then I heard her scream in agony. I managed to open my eyes a little. The monster had kicked her across the room shouting, "Get that fucking dog away from me." He lay on the bed and lit a cigarette. Indie came cowering to my side and we lay huddled together on the floor.

I was starting to realise that I was going to die if I didn't get out of that room, but my body couldn't move. After a few minutes he got off the bed and walked slowly over to me. He stood over me and then told me to get my arse ready, he was going to fuck me again. He dropped slowly to his knees, with my head in between his thighs. He was masturbating himself and telling me to get my arse ready. He leaned forward, supporting his body with his left hand laid flat on the floor and masturbating his penis over my face with the right hand. Indie ran to the doorway and I moved my head towards the ceiling. He was masturbating hard and fast, shoving his knob into my mouth then taking it out and masturbating. "Shove your dirty white tongue up my arsehole," he shouted. "Rim me, bitch, rim me." He was still masturbating hard and, just as he was about to ejaculate, out of nowhere I found strength. I had no idea where it came from but I raised my right leg and swung it right into the side of his head. He stumbled to the floor dazed and I jumped up, grabbed Indie and ran.

I tied the rope around my housecoat and ran downstairs into the bathroom. I dabbed the bleeding with a towel. I panicked a bit and ran into the back of the shop. I was wondering what I was going to do. I put some cloths on that were still damp from the morning dew, these were on the washing line at the back. I could hear him coming down the stairs and he went into the kitchen to get a beer, he then went into the lounge and put the TV on.

It was after seven. All the time I'm thinking, should I ring the police? I was scared. I'd just been beaten and raped by a lunatic. I ran with Indie to Heaton Park and aimed to get to the Temple, the highest point in Manchester. I fell several times and Indie could barely keep up. I hid in some bushes for I don't know how long. I got back to the shop before nine. He'd gone.

I had shut the shop as normal and then told Sarah I would drop her off at home. I had been on edge all day. I dropped her off in Radcliffe. As I drove back past the shop, this was at quarter to seven, I saw monster and three other black guys. They looked like they had been to the shop; they were carrying beers and were walking down Bury Old Road. The monster saw me drive past. I saw him look at my car through the car mirrors. I carried on driving and went over to Yvonne's; I spent a couple of hours there. I didn't tell her anything, I didn't tell anyone. When I came home, I parked the car round the back on the residential estate, rather than at the front of the shop like I normally do. Once inside, I locked the door and bolted everything that could be bolted.

I rang the police on Wednesday, 1st September, 2010 and reported the theft of the money. An appointment was made for two police officers to attend the following day at 15.00hrs. I spent that night thinking about it. I thought, I'm lying. I'm going to have to sit in front of these police officers and report the theft; in the grand scheme of things the theft is neither here nor there. I thought, I will have to explain the theft when there is a much more serious issue. All sorts of things were running through my mind. My injuries were worrying me, this man had physically hurt me. I was concerned about the shop, I was worried about money, I was scared the monster might come back as I'm afraid of him. I didn't want a big drama, lots of fuss and the police dragging me off for interviews. I have a new small business; I didn't want the police at the door. I wasn't in the right frame of mind.

The next day I phoned the police and explained that there was something more to what I had reported. I told them that the monster had tried to rape me. I stated that the monster had tried to rape me, because at the time my understanding of rape was that the rapist had to ejaculate inside my bum. The monster had fully penetrated me but, as far as I knew, hadn't ejaculated; the technical term by the letter of the law. I do not know, but at the time I thought this meant he had tried to rape me.

DS Gareth J. came down and we had a chat. I was struggling for courage. I remember I was annoyed with one of the forensic ladies who had come to the shop. She was stood outside the shop in broad daylight taking photographs. Stuff like that was a big thing to me, I was fuming,

I was thinking customers are walking into the shop, these two ladies dressed in uniforms, what are people going to think? I know that they were just doing their jobs but I hadn't slept properly for two weeks, my head was all over the place. The following day I went to North Manchester General Hospital A&E. I explained I had been assaulted and that I still had pain in my testicle. They examined me, told there was bruising and scabs from the bites, but the marks were healing very well.

The monster stated that his name was xxxxx, he is about 6ft, taller than me, slim but very muscular build, trendy clothes, always wearing hats or carrying a man bag. He is black, he stated his parents were from Barbados and he was from London. He is aged 20, good-looking, he stated that he lived on xxxxx Road in Radcliffe..

The first person I told was my mum.

DS Gareth J.
Greater Manchester Police
Public Protection Division
Serious Sexual Offences Unit
North Hub,
Rochdale Police Station

On first reading that transcript almost a year later, it sent me into a full episode of PTSD, but I forced myself to read it and then again and again until my PTSD subsided. Strangely though, it also made me remember Brian, my dear friend who had been murdered brutally by a homeless thug.

Brian had met the monster that first night when he invited us to have a drink at his and admire his new fish tank. He took an instant dislike to the monster and made it very clear, although he pretended to be polite. After the trial, I went to see Brian and we had a great day. We took Indie and Brian's collie dog, Bobby, to Heaton Park and spent the day mainly at the boating lake, drinking coffee and relaxing. Brian hadn't known about the rape and he was really supportive that day. He said he'd ask Noirin to pass on my thanks to Jenny McAlpine.

The last day I spent with my dear friend Brian was a hot day in August. Lisa, his neighbour and my friend, brought her dogs for grooming and calmly told me that Brian had been murdered. My PTSD kicked in immediately and Lee, as ever, was there to help.

Before Lisa left the shop, she said there would be a "viewing" at Lilywhites funeral directors on Bury Old Road. At the time I thought, why would I want to "view" my friend's body when he had been hacked to death? I didn't go to see Brian's body.

Many months later, the *Manchester Evening News* covered the story. It was on the front page, headline news. I read that article, thinking at the time that it was really impersonal and also wanting to break into whatever prison that scumbag murderer was in. I wanted to cut his throat and stab him to death, just as he had done to my dear friend, gentle if not a little naive, Brian RIP.

The article read...

Knifeman caged for murder of community champion.

A knifeman who murdered a community champion has been jailed for life. Wesley Isherwood beat and stabbed 48-year-old Brian Gavigan to death at his home on Merton Road, Prestwich, last September after becoming suspicious of his friendship with his girlfriend.

Isherwood's girlfriend, Adele Eckersley, had an entirely innocent friendship with the victim but sparked a murderous fury in the killer, who had a history of violent offending. Isherwood, 28, of Bury Old Road, Prestwich, pleaded guilty to murder and would have to serve 24 years and 192 days behind bars before he can be released. Friends of Mr Gavigan welcomed the sentence and paid tribute to him. Councillor Vic D'Albert knew Mr Gavigan when he was on the committee of the Save Heaton Park Group. He said, "Brian was a very involved member of the Heaton Park Action Group and a kind and gentle man who did a lot for the community and had a lot of friends. What happened was a tragedy and he is missed to this day."

Monsignor John Allen, the Priest at Our Lady of Grace Church where Mr Gavigan was a parishioner, also paid tribute to him. He said, "It is an occasion to renew our thoughts, prayers and sympathy with Brian's family."

Manchester Crown Court heard how hours before killing Mr Gavigan, Isherwood told him to stay away from his girlfriend and said he would kill him if he visited her again. Later that night Isherwood returned to Mr Gavigan's home where he beat him before attempting to strangle him. He then cut his throat and stabbed him in the abdomen.

The next day Isherwood confided to a friend that he had gone back to the victim's address and killed him.

Police were phoned and Isherwood was arrested. While awaiting trial for Mr Gavigan's murder, Isherwood made a chilling boast in a letter to Miss Eckersley from his prison cell. He said, "I don't feel a damn thing for him or his family. I'm glad he's dead.

"I live my life by my own rules, my own laws. When people break them, I become judge, jury and, in this case, I became executioner as well."

The day of Brian's funeral came and went. The night before, I lay in bed holding his picture and deeply contemplating my own life.

It's real, I kept thinking, me being raped and my nearly deadly brush with HIV, my little brother in a Spanish jail for murder, Mo's cancer and the surrogate babies, and my friend being brutally murdered. I should write a bloody book.

Brian's funeral was, to me, a little impersonal but I assumed that's how his family wanted it. Brian's girls, Sarah and Emma, looked just like him. I didn't see them smile but

I'd imagined that if they did, I would see their dad, my friend, Brian.

I sat with Shirley, another neighbour of ours in Prestwich, and a bit of a drinker to say the least. She gave me her permission to write about her and said she wanted to be described as "the beautiful Shirley". Brian had fancied her and she was indeed very attractive, or at least was back in the day.

Nobody stole my tears at the funeral. I could grieve openly and honestly at the sad passing of a good friend. Lisa had made a collection for the flowers from Brian's neighbours and friends. They were beautiful. She said the dickhead florist had put a pink ribbon on by mistake. That made me giggle. I wore a black outfit and my bright pink scarf, just for Brian.

Lee watched the shop for me, and afterwards I walked from Prestwich village back to Victoria Avenue, passing Brian's little house on the way. It was cordoned off still with that blue tape the police use at the scene of a crime. They'd used it outside the old shop after the rape, but I took it down when they'd gone.

When I got back to the shop, I handed Lee the mass card, or whatever it is you call them. Lee read it; it gave him goosebumps, he said. It made me cry and I read that card over and over in bed that night, crying myself to sleep in the process. It read:

"If tomorrow starts without me and I'm not there to see,
If the sun should rise and fill your eyes all filled with tears for me,
I wish so much you wouldn't cry the way you did today.
While thinking of you many times, we didn't get to say,
As much as I love you and I know you'll miss me too.
But when tomorrow starts without me please try to understand
That an Angel came and called my name and took me by the hand

And said my place was ready, in heaven, for sure
And that I'd have to leave behind all those I dearly love.
So when tomorrow starts without me, don't think we're far apart.
For every time you think of me, I'm right here in your heart.

Brian Gavigan
28th May, 1963 – 4th September, 2011
Requiscant In Pace

The monster that had murdered Brian lived at the homeless hostel just opposite the old shop. I and many of the residents had had many run-ins with the owners and the residents, but this was the final straw. We got a campaign going to shut it down. That campaign was led very much by Bettina, or Betty, my good friend and a magistrate at Manchester Magistrates Court.

Around the time of Brian's funeral, there was a report of a rape on Wild Flower meadow, a five minute walk from the new shop. The police came to see me, just checking I was "ok". The fifteen-year-old girl who had made the first allegation, was lying. She'd had consensual sex with her boyfriend, also fifteen. She panicked and lied to her parents, who in turn called the police. The other three rapes were only rumours. Rumours started through fear, real fear, but rumours nonetheless.

I asked the policeman if the girl would be punished and he looked at Lee and I rather apologetically, and said "no". No further action would be taken. Maybe she would suffer some form of natural justice, I thought. Anyway, no monster was on the loose, not that type anyway.

That meant that Lee and I could walk Indie again. We went to Blackley Woods. The weather was glorious and Indie pulled Lee a little, but he controlled her pretty well. We stopped at our favourite spot, the little "beach" next to the shallow, slow flowing river, just under the little wooden bridge. I threw stones for Indie and she "nearly" swam.

Lee had his joint in hand. Sue, a customer and local lady with her two dogs, looked on from the little bridge. She must have thought it was like a scene from Huckleberry Finn.

Lee whispered to me, "I wish she'd fuck off so I can light this joint." She did and we shared that joint.

The following weekend was a good one. Dawn had come to visit for the first time since the rape; she brought her youngest, Lorenzo, and Paddy, her Labrador cross.

When I met her at the shop, she said, "You look great," with a surprised tone to her voice.

"What were you expecting?" I replied. She didn't answer.

On the Saturday, Lorenzo, Dean Adam and Lee went to the United game at Old Trafford. It was October but the hottest day on record in the UK, ever. After the game Dawn and I met the lads and we all enjoyed a Chinese banquet, all you can eat for eight pound a head.

After the meal Lorenzo and Dean Adam got a cab back to Dean Adam's new flat in Fallowfield, and Dawn, Lee and I walked through the Gay Village to get a cab. To them it was just a walk through what Dawn said was a beautiful part of town. To me it was a walk through the monster's exclusion zone.

Joan, from Victim Liaison Service, had come to the shop to explain the restrictions on his release. She asked me what physical exclusion zones I would like her to apply for. I told her that obviously I'd like the immediate area around the new shop and the Gay Village. The following day a yellow map arrived. It had blacked out parts of Manchester. The whole of North Manchester as far as Rochdale and the Gay Village.

The following Tuesday I brought that map to the group and Duncan pointed out that the Gay Village exclusion was only, in fact, Canal Street – or Anal Treat, as it had become known.

The following morning I rang Joan and, hey presto, with the touch of a button she extended the zone to include the whole of the Village and not just "Anal Treat". That feeling of empowerment meant a lot to my ongoing recovery.

Dawn, Lorenzo and Paddy went home to Camden that Sunday and I got on with not looking forward to Christmas. There was, however, something more important than Christmas at the moment and that was the closure of the hostel where Brian's murderer had lived, and his girlfriend currently lived with all the other residents – some nice and some not so nice.

≈ 9 ≈

My Friend Betty

Bettina had provided everyone with blank petitions and a covering letter. It read:

Dear Residents,

Following the recent hideous homicide inflicted upon a well-known and well respected neighbour of Merton Road, Mr Brian Gavigan. Allegedly the person responsible for this senseless crime was a resident of xxxx Villas, xxxx Bury Old Road.

Over the years, we in the immediate community have come to the end of our patience putting up with the escapades of the residents from this establishment. Some of whom are drug users who make no effort to hide this offence especially in the car park of St Margaret's Tavern, corner of Milton and Heys Road, where they hang around waiting for their supply of drugs.

The Police are well aware of this and have been for some time. But it seems nothing has been done to close down xxxxx Villas. Over the next week, and weather permitting, a committee member will be calling with a petition which I sincerely hope you will sign, the intention being the swift closure of the above mentioned, permanently. In doing so ridding this public nuisance from our community.

Many thanks in advance

Bettina Hughes JP Chairperson.

I filled up ten petitions with about two hundred names. Many of my customers had no clue what they were signing but that was ok. I rang Bettina and she was really excited that the campaign was going well. She also had great news, her bowel cancer was in remission and she was really looking forward to taking on the hostel owners at the meeting the following Friday.

I got ready after work that Friday and walked up to Lisa's house on Milton Road. After a coffee, we walked round to the Working Man's Club on Bury Old Road. The function room was full to bursting; what a tribute to Brian, we all said. We were five minutes early. I recognised lots of old neighbours and friends and I was determined to have my say at that meeting. Before that, however, I had a much more pressing job. Where was Bettina? She was at the "top table" with a number of representatives from the police and local council, Bury. I always thought it was strange that my old shop and flat were at Three-Nine-Nine Bury Old Road, Manchester M25 1PS, and yet they were actually in Bury.

I walked up to Bettina, who gave me her usual gentle hug and kiss on the cheek, and I wanted to cry. "Great news," I whispered in her ear, "just the best news ever." She fought back the tears too and calmly composed herself whilst retaking her seat. Before I found a seat in the hall, I gave her the Angel card I had chosen for her that day from the flower shop over the road. You see, Bettina and I – and it turns out lots of other people – believe in Angels too.

Bettina's card read...

Angel of Guidance

You may not know what path to take
Or be sure what to do

And life seems full of obstacles that you can't see your
way through.
But there are angels who can help
For that's their special task.
And one will gladly help you too
You only have to ask.

I found a seat just in front of Lisa and not far from a very
pissed-up Shirley. Would you fancy her now, Brian? I thought.

Nearly all of the people at that meeting were there for
Brian. They weren't afraid of repercussions from the
scumbags in the hostel; not the deserving service users, not
them. But the ones who were plotting and scheming to
protect that monster, Brian's executioner. The monster who
threatened to smash his fish tank if he didn't give him money.
He smashed the fish tank anyway, then beat him half to death
and, that not being enough, he cut his throat, just to finish the
job. No wonder we were really angry that night.

Bettina started the proceedings by asking for a minute's
silence. She got it. Not a cough or a sneeze, just pure silence.
I cried but hid my tears. I wondered, did anyone notice me
swaying slightly? I was trying to hide my tears but I suppose
that emotion has to manifest physically. I swayed, gently, but
enough for me to notice. They didn't notice.

The minute's silence came and went but the anger grew
and grew until Bettina could no longer control things.
Everyone tried to help Bettina, even the councillors tried to
control the dickheads who came to the meeting pissed-up.

Then, amid gasps from the crowd, the owners of the
hostel slopped in and sat at the back. A couple in their fifties,
they looked like tramps, and were very clearly stoned. He tried
to answer questions fired at him but he had no clue what day
it was, let alone answer questions. She wasn't as stoned but
she was angry; an angry woman who came for a fight. She

wasn't expecting what she got. She got the truth. They showed no remorse for Brian's death.

Noirin stood up at the back. I'd tried earlier to catch her eye but I got the impression she was avoiding me, or maybe she had poor eyesight and I was just being paranoid. To my surprise, she gave them loads. She held nothing back and was trembling with anger.

Everyone had their say and I think if Bettina and the councillors hadn't been there, it would have turned into a lynch mob. The seat beside me was empty only for a few minutes, then the lovely Carol came in and sat beside me. Carol had worked with Yvonne in the Manchester Dogs Home charity shop for years. She was a loyal customer.

Carol's mixed breed dog, Harvey, had the same colour hair as hers, a lovely fiery red. Dogs do really look like their owners, or maybe when we choose a dog we look for something that we consciously or subconsciously see in ourselves. It was funny that when Carol came to ask my advice about stun collars, I told her, "Yes, it probably would stop Harvey barking but how would you like it if you got an electric shock every time you spoke out of place?"

She didn't get the collar, and slowly but surely Harvey's barking became acceptable. The irony is that Carol's deaf!

Thank God Carol had come. A couple of minutes after she sat down, Shirley walked to where I was sitting, said hi, and looked at the back of Carol's head. She curled her lip like a child, she clearly wanted to sit next to me. I said hi, she found another seat and sat down, pint in hand. I pitied the person sat next to her.

As the meeting progressed, so did the anger. The atmosphere in that room was tense, really tense. Noirin stood up and told of a previous death; no, murder. It was ten years earlier and the circumstances were similar. The drug taking, dealing, the general antisocial behaviour in the area and, most importantly, that murder had been committed by a resident of the hostel.

The hostel owners were asked by Bettina to come to the front to answer questions in a controlled manner. The room was finally under control and he took a seat at the front. After a disastrous questions and no answers session, she sloped up to join him. Her contribution was even less enlightening.

I decided to ask a few questions of my own, and for once my social work background came in handy. I threw my questions at them. What were the policies and procedures in place at the hostel? What admissions criteria were in place? Who funded and inspected them? What were their qualifications? Who was employed and what background checks were done? Who funded and inspected them? etc., etc.

I got no answers but at one point he tried to disrespect Brian's memory. That's when I lost it and, rather unexpectedly, I stood up and shouted, "Don't you fucking dare go there."

I got a round of applause, I sat down and he shut up.

Shirley decided in her pissed-up wisdom that it would be ok to verbally abuse one of the councillors. Was it his fault that Brian was dead? No, of course not; it was and is only the responsibility of the murderer. There may have been some responsibility on the part of the hostel owners, the other residents, and maybe the social workers. Most definitely some responsibility lay on the police, the police who were invited to attend but didn't. The community liaison officer stayed at home to tend to his leaky roof and sent a lovely young lady, a plastic bobby, instead. That young girl did her best. She used to have her dog groomed by me at the old shop. I gave her my new address and apologies to her on behalf of all of us; she accepted that apology.

At the end of the meeting, everyone agreed to let the councillors do their job and we would meet again in two-four weeks' time. Lisa would let everyone know the date.

I was having a cig outside the club, when one of the councillors came over to chat. "So what made you move shop?" he asked.

Here we go again, I thought, and replied, "I was raped in that shop."

"I'm so sorry, John," he said, genuinely compassionate. "So did they catch him?"

"Yes," I said. And then the obvious question came, the one I hated answering.

"Can I ask how long he got?" he said.

"You can ask, but I don't think you'll like the answer."

"Go on then," he said tentatively.

"Fifteen months, actually four years reduced to two, but yes, in total fifteen months."

"Shit," he said, shaking his head in disbelief.

I changed the subject. I told him about the time at the old shop when me and a few neighbours, including Brian, had collected the rubbish left by the hostel residents in St Margaret's churchyard. We filled a bin bag with beer bottles and cans, condoms, syringes and all sorts of shit. I marched over to the hostel and emptied that bag of shit on the lounge floor. The owner ran to the lounge, clearly stoned, and said angrily, "What the fuck are you doing, you mad bastard?" I replied calmly, "Your shit, I believe. No charge for delivery."

The councillor laughed and asked if I would do it if I'd known a brutal murderer lived there.

"Of course," I said.

I kissed Bettina goodnight and took a lift home from John, Lisa's husband. When I got home, I got a text from Shirley.

"I spoke up for Brian because, as you know, he would have spoken up for me. Stay in touch, love Shirley and Trixie."

I barely knew the woman. I rang Lisa and read her the text. We laughed out loud. I suppose the most important part of the meeting, to me anyway, was the warmth and compassion demonstrated at all levels. Not just for Brian, as many didn't know him, but for the community and each other as a whole.

The following day was an important day for me. I was going to put some demons to bed – or at least, that was the plan.

Twenty-first of December, 2011. 6.43pm and I was waiting for Neill. After a very busy day, I went upstairs to change. I left Tia, Neill's dog, in the shop. I got ready, done up to the nines, and went back downstairs to play footie with Tia whilst we waited for Neill.

Neill worked for Rob, who had bought the old shop and the place I had arranged to visit. Was my PTSD going to envelop me? I didn't know, but I needed to be strong and prove something to myself.

I had Neill's Christmas pressie in a silver and black fancy wine bag. Tia and I waited. She wasn't bad at footie, her tackle needed a bit of work but her catch was excellent. We waited and then, seven pm, Neill arrived, pressies in hand. Helen had made three different sponge tarts – chocolate, cherry and almond, and apple. They were all wrapped up and still warm, even labelled, for God's sake! Neill said Tia looked great and added very solemnly, "When you're ready, mate."

I thought, why am I doing this? But I was.

We drove the few miles up the road to the old shop. It looked the same, at first glance. The "for sale/to let" sign was still up. The shutters looked the same. Neill has put French doors where the shop window was. The main shop area looked similar, but was now a furniture store; office furniture and supplies.

The bathing room at the back looked the same, but Neill told me it now had metal shutters on the windows. We slowly rambled about the building. The message I got from Neill was that security was rock tight, metal bars on all the doors and windows, an intercom system fitted, alarm system and the whole "shebang". It felt safe.

I asked Neill to show me the basement, my "safe room". Neill led the way and I followed, walking slowly and nervously down the short dark staircase. It was a disgrace, just like when Matthew and I moved in, full to bursting with stuff – lots of stock, stationery and office furniture for their newly revamped business.

I wanted to sit in that basement, but I'm glad I didn't. Glad I only spent a moment in that still cold, dark and miserable place. Neill led the way and we slowly made our way upstairs. I could feel the anxiety starting, the pain in my stomach and my laboured breathing. I took each step slowly and we got to the first floor. We went into the tiny kitchen.

I could see him, even though he wasn't there. Cooking Jerk Chicken.

"Can we get out of here, Neill, please?"

"No probs, mate," he replied. And he led the way to the lounge.

It looked the same but had office furniture, as it was now a large multi-user office. Neill pointed out all the improvements and then I politely asked him to show me the attic, the bedroom and the place where it happened.

I took hold of the handrail leading up to the small vestibule at the entrance to the door. The short staircase, ten steps, seemed like a mountain; a mountain leading to a horror movie; a movie in which I had the leading role.

Neill led the way. "You can do it, John. Come on, mate," he said calmly and gently, and repeated it as I took the first step, then another and another, until I finally got to the door.

Neill stood in front of me and gently pushed the unlocked door open. The palpitations grew stronger and were closer together. I took a very deep breath and wrapped my arms around me, clutching at my shoulders as tightly as I could. I placed my right foot on the little step and forced myself to go inside.

"Well done, mate, you can do it," Neil said gently, in an almost whisper-like voice.

I walked to the middle of the room and there they were, the holes in the walls poorly filled with Polyfilla. "I filled those holes in," I said to Neill.

"I was wondering about them. How did they get there in the first place?" Neill asked.

"Some of them he did when punching the walls, before he..." I tried to continue. "The rest he did when he used my head and not his fists."

The palpitations became too much and I told Neill I needed to get out of that room. As we walked downstairs, my breathing started to return to normal. I'd done it, faced my demons and I didn't need an ambulance. I walked home that night and thanked my friend, Neill, profusely.

The weeks went by and, after another couple of meetings, the hostel remained open but they did clean up their act and only decent people were housed there.

I was working away with Lee in the shop one day when I got a text message from Dawn. "Da has cancer," it said.

She had tried to ring me, but either way the effect was the same. I sat on the couch in the waiting area trying to breathe and, as Lee pondered whether to call the ambulance, the mobile rang. Lee said it was Lisa and told her I couldn't speak at the moment. I struggled to breathe but I knew I had to take the call as Bettina's cancer had come back.

Lisa's crying gave it away immediately. The beautiful Bettina was dead.

"You can call that ambulance now, Lee."

Just when I thought my PTSD had subsided, it came back. I had not managed to get rid of it but I had learned to understand it. I would explain to Duncan and the lads that it was not necessarily memories or triggers of the rape that left me in such a state. It was and is anxiety *per se*.

I generally had episodes at work or at home, and the hospital, North Manchester General, knew that when the ambulance came it must not use lights or sirens as this deepened the severity of the episode. Basically I would lie down in the back of the ambulance, and the paramedics – who generally had a good understanding of my condition – would speak gently and encourage me to breathe with the aid of the oxygen mask. At the same time they would monitor my blood pressure, which usually was double what it should be.

At the hospital I would usually try to walk unaided, with a paramedic guiding me to a treatment room. I would lie down for maybe an hour, being monitored all the time, until I would be able to breathe normally. When I was ready to go, I would ask for the hospital psychiatrist, who I got to know quite well. I would reassure her that I wasn't suicidal, even if I was, and then I'd walk back home. The walking was and is an important part of my recovery from a PTSD episode.

The first time I went to the hospital was for my forensic examination and, strangely, I felt fine that day. It was a Friday and Gareth had pestered me to go as the scars were starting to fade. Yvonne picked me up and off we went. The A&E was full to bursting. There were really ill people everywhere.

I went to the counter and, when the nurse asked me what the problem was, I whispered as best I could, "I've been raped."

Just my poxy luck, she was hard of hearing.

"What did you say?" she bellowed.

I had no choice, so I composed myself and said as clearly as I could, whilst trying to manage the volume of my voice, "I have been raped."

That was it. The noisy A&E fell silent and all eyes and attention turned to me.

The nurse said, "Take a seat please, John."

I turned to face the crowd and almost closed my eyes as I did what she said and sat down. An elderly man sitting near to Yvonne and me was throwing up violently. Other people had cuts, bruises, gashes, fevers and really were ill. I felt fine, physically anyway.

Within about five minutes of me sitting down, a doctor came through the double doors and called out my name. Another reason for the other people in the waiting area to either snigger or just stare. I could only imagine some of the conversations around dinner tables that evening. "John Lennon's been raped. Imagine."

I walked over to the doctor and said, "Surely some of the other patients needed attention before me."

"No," she said, "we'd like to see you first."

This was to become a regular thing; I got priority at the hospital each time I attended. On this particular occasion, the lady doctor asked me to sit on the examination bed and then asked me something which, at the time, I thought was a little strange. "Would you prefer a male doctor?"

I've pondered about this many times. Here I was in a place of safety and I wondered, what difference does it make? I suppose, to some people it might matter, but to me a doctor is a doctor. I was raped by a man but had I been raped by a woman it wouldn't have made a difference. I told the doctor I had no preference and she went off, leaving me to undress.

She came back with another doctor – a man – and they examined me. That examination, both external and internal, was horrible; cold and calculated. They used a fabric measuring tape to measure the size of my scars and bruises.

She even measured the size in centimetres of the bite marks, which hadn't faded but had scabbed over.

"How could anybody do such a thing?" the lady doctor said, whilst shaking her head in disbelief.

"I don't know," I replied. "But he did it."

I tried to make as light of the situation as possible and, as the doctor measured the bite on my penis, I said, "You're going to need a bigger measuring tape." Neither of them laughed.

The male doctor asked if it was okay for him to take some photographs. I told him that was fine and off he went to get a camera. He came back a few minutes later and explained to the lady doctor and me that the hospital camera was broken. I couldn't fucking believe it. Had the NHS deteriorated that much that they couldn't get a poxy camera fixed?

He asked if I had a camera on my phone, and I said yes.

"We'll just have to use that then," he said. And so we did.

I left that hospital with crucial evidence in a high profile rape case, on a £20 Tesco mobile. That evidence would later be used to convict the monster in court.

The day I got the news about Bettina and Plumbob, the episode of PTSD lasted all day and I was finally released from the hospital at 1am. I walked home.

The days came and went, and it was finally the day to pay our last respects to Bettina.

I woke at 7.18am. I didn't sleep well the previous night, worrying about Dad's second scan today – a PET scan, whatever that is. Bettina had asked for contributions to Christie's rather than flowers, but I was thinking of bringing a single flower. Lisa collected £90 for Christie's.

I got dressed: pinstriped black pants, black shirt and jacket, and my bright pink scarf. I was to meet Lisa and the others at 11.30am at Blackley Crematorium, just over the road.

The forecast said light winds and rain; not bad for January, I thought. On the way to the cemetery, I popped into the Flower Spot and bought a single red rose. Christine gave me a little card, and on it I wrote, "Bettina, you were and are an inspiration to me."

Bettina got a good turnout – lots of familiar faces, friends, neighbours, sympathetic smiles, genuine and not so genuine hugs and kisses. I sat with Lisa in the second row. I couldn't see Sean or Shirley, but Brenda was sitting by Stephen's side. Dear Brenda, Bettina's best friend for over forty years. Brenda was visibly upset but she looked proud, proud to have been her friend.

The service was very personal. I discovered loads about my friend. Bettina had worked at a mill at only fifteen, she became the PA to the owner two years later, she then went to work at Boots and later decided to become a magistrate. She had told me about many of the cases she had worked on. She gave a man the maximum two years in jail for beating his dog, and on a separate occasion she let a man go scot-free; this man had bitten the tip off a copper's finger. Bettina explained that the man's defence was that the police had left him in the back of a police van for six hours; she thought this was wrong, so she let him go.

Before my monster's trial, she reckoned he would get at least eight years. She said if she had been the Judge, he would have got life.

At the service, I spotted Shirley and, after a very long look, I decided she was not as sexy as Brian had thought. She looked like the Joker from Batman, with all that make-up.

The cremation was quick; too quick in my opinion, but she wouldn't have wanted a fuss. There was one hymn, it was nice, and the lady vicar talked about what it meant to Bettina and Stephen. It meant nothing to me.

At the end of the service they played Tina Turner's *"Simply the Best"*. We cried, giggled and danced at the same time. When I spoke to Lisa later, she was a bit pissed off.

Shirley, the Joker, had said to her that Stephen had shown no emotion at the funeral and that he was a pisshead. Lisa wanted to say, "And what the fuck are you?" But she maintained her usual grace and dignity; it was a funeral, after all. I'd have knocked her out.

Lisa and I joked about Bettina's will. I wanted her gavel but with my luck, I'd end up with the fifteen-year-old, blind Jojo, their Cavalier King Charles Spaniel. We laughed and tried not to cry during that conversation.

Later that night Lisa rang and told me that my single red rose was taken to a hospice, along with the huge bouquet from Stephen, and a smaller one from "The Kids". I'm now hoping my message on that card will bring some comfort to someone. Bettina was, and always will be, an inspiration to me.

≈ 10 ≈

Crown Court

The following day I got a call from Linda. Dad has cancer, this time for sure. Lung cancer in both lungs but they don't think it's "aggressive". How could any form of cancer not be aggressive? I did and still do wonder.

Around the same time of getting the news about Dad's cancer, Jackie asked me could I go to Manchester Crown Court for the opening day of Kelly's monster's trial.

Just after my monster's trial, a customer called Allima introduced me to Jackie (name changed for protection), now a close friend. Her daughter, just fifteen, had been raped by a man she had trusted – Jackie's partner of ten years. I saw this as a challenge for my PTSD and I wanted to support her, so I asked Simon if he'd come with me as, if my PTSD kicked in, I would need someone there to support me.

She had come to see me in work the previous Saturday and asked what I had worn at "my" trial. I asked her what she wanted to wear at "hers" and she very calmly said "pyjamas". Jackie said very firmly that she wouldn't be wearing any such thing but I reassured her that she should wear whatever she felt comfortable in. Before she left the shop, she asked me to wear my black outfit and my bright pink scarf for her monster's trial the following Monday.

"Of course I will," I said.

Monday morning came and I got ready. Black from head to toe, with pointed black boots with a bit of a heel, my black trilby hat and, of course, my scarf. My hair had grown really long and I'd had highlights put in.

I met Simon at the court in Crown Square at 10am. As we waited outside court room eleven, an usher came round and took our names and asked us who we were there to support.

That day I had decided to dress to confuse. From a distance, I could have passed for a woman. I even went as far as wearing a pale red lipgloss and had my eyebrows and lashes tinted dark brown. My point to the jury, who I had instructed the usher to inform, was that I was also a rape victim – male, female, adult or child, rape is rape, full stop.

Simon and I took our seats in the public gallery. I kept my PTSD at bay until they brought Rat Face to the dock. Rat Face was what we called him, as he did in fact look like a rat; a sad, grey, pale-faced, mealy-mouthed rat.

The charges were read out. I couldn't listen but I was aware I couldn't leave the public gallery. I also could not break any of the "rules" of Crown Court; rules I was only too aware of. My PTSD kicked in but I had to be strong for Kelly.

At one point throughout that most horrible of days, Simon squeezed my hand so hard my "hairdresser's hand" popped. The pus sprayed onto the two women sitting in front of Simon and me. His sister and his new partner were there to support Rat Face.

The physical pain in my hand didn't bother me but the pain, emotional pain at what I was hearing made my PTSD much worse and, luckily, a break was ordered by the Judge. I ran like the wind through Manchester Crown Court and finally got outside to breathe. I paced and breathed the fresh air and Simon angrily text, and the concept of "No Means No" was born.

We returned to the courtroom. We listened to the charges in full. The Rat was accused of five counts of rape, child abuse, voyeurism and whatever else that Rat did. To my surprise, the Rat had also been accused by his biological daughter. The Rat remained calm and controlled in that dock whilst we and the jury recoiled in horror at what we were hearing.

Again, to my surprise, he was not held behind bullet-proof glass, as my monster was, but he was handcuffed to two prison officers in an open dock. After lots of swearing in and legal arguments, the Judge scheduled the case for a full week but warned the jury that it could go on longer.

In my case, Sue, the witness care manager, called Friday, verdict day. However my monster received his verdict on a Monday. The week went on and both Kelly and Jackie were called not once, but recalled twice, for cross-examination. Jackie gave her evidence without the aid of screens – a decision she would later regret – and Kelly gave hers using video link.

Friday came and I went to work with Lee. Jackie called me at about 1pm. She cried down the phone, "Guilty, guilty, guilty!" I screamed with delight.

The Rat got eleven years and life on the Sex Offenders' Register and the following Saturday, the *Manchester Evening News* covered the story. It read...

Disgraced War Hero Who Raped Teenage Girl Is Jailed

Pervert claimed he was incapable of sex attacks

A shamed hero soldier has been jailed for sex offences despite claiming that he couldn't have abused two schoolgirls because Gulf War Syndrome made him impotent. Michael XX was commended for bravery and leadership after he ran into a hail of bullets and shells to help the wounded during the 1990 war in Bosnia. But now he has been jailed for eleven years after a Manchester Crown Court Jury found him guilty of rape, sexual assault, sexual touching, voyeurism and assault dating back to 2010.

XX lured an underage girl into his bedroom before sexually assaulting and raping her. He had physically assaulted her on a previous occasion, the court heard.

His second victim, also an underage teenage girl, was touched, leered at and spied on by XX, who made sleazy remarks about her body shape but told her, "I'm not a pervert."

XX had denied all the offences saying there was "no truth" in the "disgusting" allegations. He had told the jury he had showed symptoms of Gulf War Syndrome since serving in the conflict in 1990 and it is understood he had been formally diagnosed with the condition. The disorder has painful and debilitating symptoms and can leave sufferers impotent.

Giving evidence in court, XX said he was "no longer a sexual person" listing other physical complaints that would prevent him from assaulting either girl. But the jury rejected his claims and returned unanimous guilty verdicts.

The court heard that the former Lance Corporal of XXXX Avenue, XXXX, served all over the world during his seventeen year career. But, after returning to civilian life his mental and physical health sharply declined.

He has been diagnosed with post-traumatic stress disorder as a result of his experiences in Sarajevo, and manic depression, worsened by drug abuse, boozing and his failure to take medication.

Richard English, defending said, "At the time Mr XX was unwell. He doesn't seek in any way to use that as an excuse but it seemed the events the victims have complained of coincided with a change in mood and disengagement from mental health services."

Sentencing, Judge David Stockdale said, "You were commended in 1993, probably in part of your active service you now suffer a genuine psychological disorder, a complex disorder. In particular you suffer manic depression. Your psychological disorder in no way excuses or explains your offending against these two young girls and does not require me to pass an order under the Mental Health Act."

Lee and I read this article in work. "You're not fucking impotent, that's for sure."

"No," I replied, "and I don't go round raping kids either."

What angered Kelly most about the *Manchester Evening News* report was the use of the work "lured". She felt that it almost implied she was a willing participant, when the truth was that the Rat dragged her to that room kicking and screaming. Kelly does, and always will, hold a special place in my heart, as will her mother, Jackie.

Since the rape, I travelled to both Dublin and Malaga quite a lot, even more than I would have done during my twenty odd years in Manchester. Of course this was because Wayne was in prison in Malaga, and because my beloved dad became seriously ill.

The first time I went to Malaga to see Wayne was actually during the trial. I'd finally given evidence and been cross-examined by the defence, but the trial was still very much on, as we had no verdict or sentence.

After that cross-examination, in full PTSD episode, I walked, as best I could, back to the witness suite with the lovely Mel. They were all waiting – Duncan, Gareth, Sue and Gail. I fell into a shivering mess on the floor, before climbing onto a chair. I'd done it. I'd given evidence and it didn't matter to me what the outcome was at that point. I'd done it.

Mel made me a coffee and everyone, especially Gail, who of course had been in the public gallery, said how well I did. I didn't have much recollection of the previous four or five hours, but she said I did really well.

Gareth sat beside me and calmly said, "You'll need that holiday now, John."

"What holiday?" I asked, genuinely confused.

"Aren't you going to Malaga tomorrow for a holiday?"

This made me angry and I shouted at Gareth, "It's not a fucking holiday. How many times? I'm going to see my brother in prison."

That night I got a police escort home and finally I could talk to my friends and family, the "witnesses", about the case.

Yvonne called me that morning before she drove to Bolton. We weren't actually allowed to discuss the case but, human nature being what it is, she told me what she was going to say.

"I'll just tell the truth," she said. She told me that she'd rung Sue, who reassured her that the TV crews would not be there. This was important to Yvonne, so she confidently went to court and gave her evidence.

She'd had her long blonde hair done, and wore a long black, loose-fitting cardigan over white three-quarter length leggings. After she gave her evidence she, unlike me, had to use the main court entrance. She rang me in a blind panic from her car.

"No cameras?" she screamed down the phone. "There was fucking flash photography waiting for me."

"Oh my God," I replied, confused, as I had made it clear that there were to be no reporters outside the court.

Yvonne got to mine, she was fuming.

"Did the cameras get you?" I asked.

"I don't think so," came the reply. "The minute I saw them, I put my cardi' over my head like Dracula and ran to my car."

"Did they follow you?" I asked.

"I think so," she said. "But I gave them the slip."

"Thank God," I said.

Yvonne rang Sue. Sue reassured her that the cameras were not there for my case, they were in fact there for a high profile paedophile case involving the abuse of twenty-eight children. That monster ran a chippy in Bury and he received a life sentence.

At one point during my trial I was being taken, yet again, through the "secret" corridors of Bolton Crown Court. The monster was being moved around again, I presumed, to give evidence. Mel and two police officers looked for a room to put me in, but they were all occupied. We came to a room I'd recognised from my pre-court visit; it was another witness suite but the one for children.

This room had miniature furniture and kids' paintings on the wall, just like a primary school room complete with toys and a television.

"We'll wait in here," Mel said. "Shouldn't be too long, John."

I sat on the edge of one of the little tables, exhausted. I hadn't noticed at first that Mel and I were not alone in that room. That room was guarded by two officers, who acted like bouncers at the door.

At the back of the room stood a little boy, possibly seven or eight years old. He wrapped his arms around the thighs of a woman who didn't appear to be his mother. She looked official, possibly a social worker.

I looked at that little boy, confused, but managed a little smile. He didn't smile back; he was petrified with fear.

"Get me out of here!" I told Mel.

"Ok, I understand," she replied. And they took me downstairs in the deliveries lift, where I had a cigarette.

I later discovered that that little boy was one of the victims in that paedophile case and he was frightened of me, just like the lady at St Mary's.

Yvonne and I discussed that little boy that afternoon. We waited for North West Tonight at 5.30pm. I couldn't wait to see her exiting the court, I thought it was hilarious. Yvonne was shitting herself that she would be on the news, particularly now as she knew she would be associated with a paedophile ring and she'd covered her face, which would kinda be seen as an admission of guilt.

We waited, listened to new and old R&B, and we danced. After dinner, on it came, North West Tonight. The paedophile case was the headline but Yvonne was okay, they hadn't shown her leaving the court.

"Thank fuck!" she said.

The following Monday I went to Malaga to see my baby brother. Each of my three musketeers – Gail, Duncan and Gareth – said they would ring me if we had a verdict. I told Gail I would only be answering calls from her, as I felt she should be the one to give me the news, be it good or bad.

I got Newco to take me to the airport. The driver asked me what the verdict was and, like everyone else, I told him I didn't know. My anxiety was at its highest ever level and the paranoia was huge. After seeing so many cameras and reporters outside the court, none of whom I spoke to, I felt I was being followed everywhere.

I got to the airport at 4am and took my seat on the EasyJet flight. I had a window seat near the front of the plane. A nice lady about my age and her son, a lad of about ten, took their seat next to me. Inevitably, we got chatting.

"Where are you from?" I asked her.

"Bolton," she replied. "Do you know Bolton?"

"Not really," I said, "but I do know the Crown Court."

That lady then excitedly went on to explain that there was a big high profile case going on at the moment.

"Oh, really," I said. "So what's it about?"

"I'm told a man was raped by some black guy."

Of course she didn't say rape, but mouthed the word whilst covering her little boy's ears.

"So what were you in court for?" she asked.

"I am that man," I calmly replied.

We didn't chat much after that, apart from the odd mention of the weather in Manchester and Malaga.

The flight landed and I did the usual baggage reclaim and security stuff before making my way to the exit. Clive, Nathan's brother, was picking me up. He said he'd wait in the little coffee shop just outside Arrivals.

I got to the automatic doors and then froze on the spot. There were TV crews everywhere. They couldn't be for me, could they?

I ran to the toilets and called Clive. No answer. I went into an empty cubicle and waited there. About an hour later, Clive called. "I'm outside, mate," he said, "been here for ages."

I told him to check that the cameras were gone.

"No, they're still here, waiting for the United players. They play Malaga tomorrow."

I knew I was paranoid, but this had been taking things to a new level.

I got myself together and went outside to meet a smiling Clive. Pearl had given birth to her new baby boy, as yet unnamed, that very morning. Clive drove a blacked-out VW Golf to the hospital where we were to meet Mum and Megan.

On the way to the hospital, Clive said he'd put a request in to the local radio station, welcoming me to Malaga. His friend, apparently, was a DJ at the station. He drove like a madman on the motorway and then, on it came: "We at Malaga FM would like to welcome Paul Lennon to sunny Malaga."

I looked at Clive, confused. "Paul?" I said.

"Oh shit, I always get you two mixed up."

"I'm nothing like him," I replied. "He's much older than me."

We got to the hospital grounds and I looked in the car mirror to check my new long blond hair. It was nearly forty degrees so I'd prepared by wearing a vest top, white canvas trousers and a white shirt. I had my man bag with a gift for the new arrival.

Nathan met us at the hospital door and I walked, flanked by Nathan and Clive, through the long corridors until we got to Pearl's room. The corridor had grown men at each door, watching me. Some turned their heads away when I looked in their direction and some cried.

"Why are they crying?" I asked Nathan. He, too, had tears in his eyes.

He replied, "They're all happy. They've just had babies."

We both knew that wasn't true. Then, from the opposite side of the corridor, came my mum and Megan. My mum, whose statement had been read in court. It was a very short statement that Gareth had taken over the phone. It read:

"I am John Lennon's mother. My son told me he was raped. I was the first person he told. My son is not a liar."

Mrs Veronica Lennon.

I hugged Mum and Megan. I was trying not to be emotional but Mum cried. "Well done," she said. "It doesn't matter what the verdict is, you've done it."

"It matters to me, Mum," I whispered in her ear.

Nathan opened the door to Pearl's room and there they were, an exhausted new mum and her perfect little boy.

"Hold him," she said. So I reached into his cot and cradled him in my arms.

We got onto the subject of names and Pearl said she and Nathan had been talking and decided, if it was okay with me, to call him John.

"No," I said. "You can't inflict that on him. Call him something nice."

I asked Faith to look in my bag and get the little gift I'd had wrapped specially for our new addition to the family. Faith unwrapped it and handed me the antique silver spoon I'd had for years.

"Keep it safe," I told Pearl, "it may be worth something one day."

One of the sentinels in the corridor knocked on the door and popped his head in. "We've got to go, now."

I said my goodbyes to Pearl and the kids, got my man bag and walked to the door.

"Sunny," Pearl said.

"Sunny what?" I asked.

"That's his name, Sunny."

"Sunny Lennon. Perfect, Pearl," I replied, and went outside to a waiting entourage.

Nathan told Clive to get us to the prison. Visiting was at half past five and it was now four thirty. Mum, Megan and I climbed into another blacked-out Golf and Clive drove.

He said he'd take the scenic route through the mountains to Al Ahuirn. He drove like a maniac and we didn't mind at first, but as the journey became dangerous, I screamed at him, "Slow down, James Cunt, my mother's being fucked about like a rag doll."

Megan thought it was all great fun. Clive slowed down a bit but it was now five o'clock and, disaster, we were lost. "I've only been up once," was Clive's defence.

We drove through lots of small villages, asking for directions. But, would you believe it, nobody spoke a word of English. I'd done the Irish equivalent of O and A level Spanish, but for the life of me I couldn't remember the word for prison. Finally, after another few disastrous attempts at getting directions, I remembered it "La penitentaria".

We stopped an old Spanish man and immediately he pointed us in the right direction. We were only a few minutes away and it was "only" five twenty-five. Clive dropped us at the gates and in we went – me, Mum and Megan; none of us having a clue what to expect.

The main waiting area was full to bursting with tired, hot and fed-up Spaniards, all waiting to hand their passports through the small hatch to the prison officer, who clearly did not want to be there. It was chaos; people shouting in Spanish, trying their best to get to see their loved ones.

I'd visited many people over the years in various prisons in Ireland and Manchester, but there was none of the organisation or control in this prison. It was almost like a lottery. I kept thinking, are we going to get to see him or not?

We waited, went outside to the now much cooler atmosphere for yet another cigarette and put our valuables in our locker, then "Wayne Lennon" was called out. We rushed to the security station and went through the same checks as you would find at any airport. We, with about thirty others, were led into a large room with prisoner art on the walls and a huge iron gate. On the ceiling there was a huge red glass light. We waited again for about half an hour then the red light became a flashing alarm; really loud, as if someone had just escaped. I couldn't bear that alarm, but luckily it indicated that we were about to go through the gates into the well-kept exercise yard.

Mum, Megan and I tentatively went through the gates and followed the crowd, all of whom seemed to know where they were going.

We huddled together, walking really slowly. Mum noticed that the people at the front entered the stairway at the base of the watch tower.

"Why are they going up there?" she asked.

I looked up, and there were two armed guards at the top of the tower. "I can't imagine why, Mum," I replied.

"Sure, I'll never make it up there," Mum declared.

"Why, Mum?" I asked.

"Have you seen these heels?" she said, laughing.

Megan and I were in stitches. Why she had worn six inch stilettos I'll never know, but she had. As we got closer to the tower, Mum squeezed my hand and said rather sadly, "Son, isn't it like that programme, *Banged Up Abroad?*"

I looked at her, a little confused, and said, "Mum, it is banged up abroad. We're in bleeding Malaga."

Again we all laughed. Maybe it was nervous laughter, as we were about to visit my baby brother, Mum's son and Megan's dad.

We got to the stairs at the entrance to the tower. Mum carried her shoes and up we went. It wasn't long before we realised that we only had to climb two short flights of stairs before we were directed in the direction of the visiting area. This was a long, long corridor with what can only be described as telephone box-style booths on one side of a glass wall, and of course the prisoners on the other side.

I had already talked with Mum and Megan about having some private time with Wayne. They were to go in first then I would have my time with him. We waited for a few minutes and found the numbered booth we were told he would be at, but there were no prisoners yet. The place was filthy and the stench of body odour overwhelming.

We decided to wait in the little booth with only one small plastic chair. Mum sat down and Megan and I peered through the glass looking for Wayne. All of a sudden another poxy siren sounded, then all hell broke loose. A stampede of tanned men of all ages came flooding from a door, all frantically looking for their visitors.

All the prisoners took their seats at the appropriate booth and then the noise. Spanish, predominantly; shouting, crying, arguing, banging on the glass. It was mayhem, but no Wayne.

Then, as we were giving up hope of seeing him, in came Wayne. The big Dublin gangster and alleged murderer? No. Just my baby brother, hobbling on crutches, looking tired and drawn. He found our booth and managed a smile, his eyes filled with tears.

He didn't take his seat at first, but laid his palm flat on the window. I covered his palm with mine and said, "I love you." Then I went outside to the corridor, leaving Mum and Megan with Wayne.

In the corridor, I came to a harsh realisation. Here I was visiting my brother in a Spanish jail, whilst I was waiting for the verdict in my own monster's trial. Surely some of the prisoners I could see and hear were sex offenders or rapists.

I scanned up and down the row. Time for another game, are you or are you not a rapist? I snapped out of it when Mum and Megan came out after maybe ten minutes and said I could go in. Wayne was now sitting and held an old-fashioned phone handle to his ear. I had to speak into a small hole in the shelf at the base of the bulletproof glass window.

"How you doing?" I asked.

"I'm holding up," he replied.

"What's happening with your leg?" was my next question. But he didn't get a chance to reply. That poxy siren again. It meant time up!

Mum and Megan rushed back in and they both told him that they loved him through teary eyes. As Wayne stood up on one crutch, so did I, slowly, trying to mimic him. He again placed his open palm on the glass and I placed mine in his. I love you, I mouthed, staring into his watery eyes and he mouthed the same.

"We'll get you out of here, I promise," I said, but he couldn't hear me. He hobbled back towards the door he'd come through and we left.

Clive met us outside the prison and he brought us to Pearl and Nathan's beautiful house on the golf course overlooking the sea. We settled in, unpacked, freshened up and discussed our plans for the evening. We decided to have dinner at Pearl's little bar in the old part of Benalmadena. I'd not heard from Gail, so I assumed the jury was still out. No verdict then.

Just as we were getting ready to leave, Nathan said we had to wait for Juan, Wayne's solicitor. He wanted to see us to discuss the case. Juan had been recommended – the best in Spain, they said.

He got to the house at 8pm, dressed in colourful flowery shorts and an open, short-sleeve shirt. He was young and good-looking and very loud. Not your typical solicitor's appointment, I thought.

He'd only just taken the case on, so his "update" wasn't much of an update. He did, however, reassure us that he would do his best for Wayne. Before he left, Mum gave him five thousand Euro and Nathan another two. Later we would discover that Juan was, in fact, a bent solicitor.

As a family, and with help from friends around the world, we'd paid him twenty-six thousand Euro, which he stole.

On my second trip to visit Wayne, Pearl, Lee and I would try to hunt down Juan in an effort to get some of that money back.

That week in Malaga was pretty uneventful. We had some meals out and tried to entertain the kids as best we could while Pearl nursed Sunny in hospital. I did lots of walking on the various beaches and watched my phone like a hawk.

Gail didn't call. How could the jury be taking so long? I wondered. Sunday came and it was time for me to go back to Manchester, leaving Mum and Megan who were staying on;

Mum for a week and Megan for the entire summer. Before I left, Pearl, who had come home with Sunny the previous Thursday, said she wanted to make Sunday lunch for all of us.

As we were preparing the meal, Michelle rang Mum's mobile. She said the *Sunday World* had run another story about Wayne. Nathan called Clive and told him to get a copy of the paper. Clive said that the only shop that sold it on the Costa del Sol had closed down.

"Don't come back without it," Nathan told him firmly.

Just as we were about to sit down to eat, in burst Clive, proudly waving a copy of the paper. "Managed to get hold of one," he said, almost out of breath.

He handed me the paper and everyone gathered round waiting for me to open it on page eight, the page Michelle told us the article was on. Just before I started to open the paper, I and everyone, couldn't help but read the headline story. There was a picture of two pretty blonde Irish girls sitting back-to-back in Dublin rugby shirts. They were smiling. The headline said "Gang raped in Cyprus".

Mum leaned forward and said, "What, the whole gang was raped?"

Of course, everyone wanted to burst out laughing but strangely nobody did.

"No, Mum," I said, "just the two girls." I wonder to this day, were they raped at all?

I opened the paper on page eight. Top right corner, Michelle had said. But in this Spanish version of the same newspaper, there was no article about Wayne, just some story about a bank robbery in Dublin. Could Michelle have got it wrong?

Pearl checked on the internet, and sure enough there it was on page eight of the Irish edition of the paper. I learned something about journalism that day.

We enjoyed our lunch that day, despite what we'd read. Pearl made her now-famous mussels in white wine sauce and paella. That night I went to a couple of bars on the seafront with Mum.

Over drinks Mum apologised for her gaff. She'd used the "R" word and I still wasn't ready to hear it; maybe that's why nobody laughed at what I now re-tell as a joke. Not a joke about rape, even though it is, but just a joke.

We made the most of that night, Mum and I, and we talked about the sentence and how long he would get. Strangely, we never discussed whether or not he would be found not guilty because I knew he was guilty. Not guilty was not an option.

Nathan took me to the airport and, as we hugged on the pavement, he told me to ring to let them know I got home safely.

"I'll ring you when I have a verdict," I told him.

≈ 11 ≈

The verdict

The following Monday I had arranged to meet Duncan at Costa Coffee in Piccadilly. The monster had been remanded in custody for trying to abscond from the court during the trial. That day I was looking out of the window in the witness suite right at the top of the court building. I'd asked if the window could be opened as I was having trouble breathing. Mel said that the windows on this floor were permanently locked. "So witnesses won't try to commit suicide?" I asked. "Yes" was her reply.

As I looked out the window I could see Gareth outside the court building. He was directing police cars like a crazy traffic controller in Times Square. "What's Gareth doing?" I asked. Gail told me that the monster had run off after the morning's questioning. "Don't worry," she calmly reassured me, "Gareth will get him." And he did, within a couple of hours. From that day, he was in prison and I could safely walk the streets; no need for my Duncan hat any more.

I got ready and headed for the tram. As I got to Blackley Woods, the phone rang. It was Gail. My heart stopped and I couldn't answer it. Just at that moment I realised that it may not be a guilty verdict, it could have all gone wrong and the reality hit me hard. I didn't answer the phone but went into the woods instead. I walked through the woods to my and Lee's "Huckleberry Finn" spot and lit a cig.

I composed myself, took a deep breath and called Gail. She answered straight away. "Well?" I asked. "Guilty," came the short reply. I told her I would call her back. I sobbed uncontrollably at that little stream. Was I crying tears of joy or relief, or was it both? I don't know but I knew I was the victor. The monster had won only one battle but I had won the war.

I called Gail back when I finally took it in and she said, "Well done, you did it," but that wasn't enough. I had one burning question. "Was it a unanimous verdict, Gail?" I asked. "I don't know the details," she said, and that I should call Sue at the court.

I called Sue immediately, she told me that the jury had indeed returned a unanimous verdict and that they wanted to meet me after the sentencing in a week's time. When I called Gail to tell her the news, she said she'd never heard of a jury wanting to meet the victim.

I continued with my journey into town, all the time digesting this hugely significant news. I'd tell everyone later but at that moment the most important person to hear my news was Duncan. I met him at Costa Coffee and, rather bewildered, I shared my news. "Did you ever doubt it would be guilty?" he asked. "No," I replied, "never for a split second did it ever cross my mind."

When I got home that day I decided to "celebrate". I bought a really nice bottle of Merlot and started to make the phone calls. The first person I rang, of course, was my mum. I must have made a hundred calls that night and halfway through making them I went to the shop to get another bottle of that Merlot. When I was finally incoherent, I decided to stop telling people and to just sit with Indie and contemplate the enormity of what I had achieved. I'd put a rapist in jail. Wow, I thought, still not quite believing it. I spent the rest of that night enjoying the wine and wondering what the hell I was going to say to the jury. Thank you, I suppose was the obvious thing. I also planned to apologise to them individually. My apology was going to be for them having to listen to the horrible details of the rape, and also for them having to see those graphic photos of my genitalia. I wondered, that night, what would they say to me in one week's time at the sentencing.

The day of sentencing arrived. I'd been warned that the cameras were there and that I would have to use the side entrance as per usual. Gareth rang and offered to send a squad car but somehow I felt free and liberated, and I told him I'd get the train and make my own way. Gail was in Tenerife so I met Mel at the side entrance to the court. We waited for what seemed a lifetime, and then a strange thing happened. My PTSD kicked in good style. I couldn't understand it; I should have felt relaxed and jubilant but my anxiety was again on high alert. It got to lunchtime and the court was adjourned.

I couldn't believe it. What the fuck was taking so long? I told Mel I wasn't in a fit state to go for lunch or even a coffee, and asked would she wait with me in the witness suite, which she did. I stared at the clock in that room as I had done many, many times during the trial. It got to two pm and I got prepared to go to the court room to see him sentenced. That was the plan, however on this occasion I really couldn't walk and I wasn't going to crawl as I'd done so many times.

Mel said she would go to the sentencing and that I should wait in the witness suite. Just before she left to go, there was a commotion in the room. Everyone was getting excited and people started tidying the room frantically. I couldn't understand what was happening and then, silence. A grey-haired man in a suit came into the room. I was struggling to breathe and panted heavily, but I recognised the man who commanded so much respect. He made a coffee at the little kitchen area and glanced in my direction. "Is that the Judge?"

I asked Mel. "Yes," she said, "he wanted to see your PTSD for himself before sentencing."

The judge left quite abruptly; another first I was later told. Judges never visit the witness suite, not in Bolton anyway. Mel followed him and I was left with another lady from the witness care team. An hour passed then two, then three. I'd just about given up and decided to go home when a very sombre Mel came back with Geoff, "my" Barrister.

Geoff knelt in front of me and gently took my hand. I was a bit more composed and I looked directly into his eyes which were filled with tears. "How long, Geoff? Is it life like I was promised?" Geoff wiped his eyes and shook his head slowly from side to side. His lips were quivering and, still holding my hand, he said, "Four years, John, that's the best I could get." "How long will he do?" I asked, trying to hide my anger. "Fifteen months," came the reply.

Mel put her arm around me as I cried openly. I eventually composed myself and Mel brought me a coffee. "It's not your fault," I said to Geoff, "you did your best." Then Geoff asked me a question I would be asked many times afterwards, "Would you do it again, John?" "What?" I asked. "Report the man who raped me?" "Yes," said Geoff. I thought about it for a moment, my PTSD episode had almost subsided and I looked Geoff right in the eye and said, "You bet your fucking life I would."

I said my goodbyes to everyone in the witness suite and there was just one more thing to do. Meet the jury.

I walked calmly, not speaking a word on the way, with Mel to the courtroom. We got to the door I was not allowed to use during proceedings; the normal door that non-victims use. Mel held the door open, I took a deep breath and went in nervously and filled with emotion. The first thing I saw was the Judge's bench but no Judge. I slowly turned my head and there they were, all twelve. They were standing and smiling sympathetically at me, some crying. I said to that jury, my jury,

"Thank you forever and from the very bottom of my heart." One lady broke down and was comforted by an older man to the left of her.

"Who was the spokesperson?" I asked through my tears. "Me," a young man replied. "It was me." "When you gave the verdict, what was the monster's reaction?" I further questioned. That young man grabbed the rail in front of him, held his head low then slowly raised it and said, "He had to be restrained by the prison officers. He screamed and banged his fists wildly on the glass, he said that it was all lies and that one day he would..." the young man paused and gulped. "Please continue," I said. "Kill you," he finished.

I took my time replying to him, took a few gulps of my own and said with a smile, "Well, I best make the most of the next fifteen months then, eh?" Everyone laughed including me, and then I received a huge round of applause. I returned the applause and, when the clapping had stopped, I said to the jury, "You're excused now, you can all go home."

≈ 12 ≈

Lost in Malaga

As the weeks and months passed, the time came for another trip to Spain. This time I was much stronger and I asked Lee if he would like to come with me. We planned our trip and the day came. Another 6am flight on Easyjet.

Carla, a customer who had become a good friend, said she would give us a lift to the airport. It was October, freezing and horrible in Manchester, but Pearl had told me they were having a record heatwave in Malaga. Carla picked us up and off we went to Manchester Airport, collecting Lee on the way.

We got to the drop off zone at Departures and, before exiting the car, I checked out my long blond hair in the mirror.

"Jesus, Carla!"

"What?" she asked, a little shocked.

"You could have told me I looked like Freddie Boswell! Look at me fucking hair."

Roaring with laughter, Carla told me she had something for me.

"What's that?" I asked curiously.

"I've written a poem for and about you," she said, and handed me a folded-up piece of A4 paper.

Carla's poem reads...

John
I know a man who baths my dogs.
Who walks about in black croc clogs.
He stands about chatting with a fag in his hand
While poor Lee works till he can barely stand.
This man I know, he's loving and kind.
He's endured so much but is strong of mind
With a mouth so foul, yet a heart so big
And his laughing face and his curly wig.
John, with your ready ear and your cups of tea
Have you any idea what a friend you are to me?

We said our ta-ras and eventually we boarded the plane. Clive was picking us up and we were staying with him and his two kids.

Lee and I got settled on the flight and, just as we were opening our seatbelts, the pilot came on over the tannoy and started speaking. Lee, sitting in the window seat, was still half-asleep and rested his head on his arm, which acted like a pillow on the little tray attached to the back of the seat in front.

The pilot said, "Good morning, folks, and welcome to what we are hoping will be a calm flight to Malaga. We are now travelling at ten thousand feet and four hundred miles per hour. The weather in Malaga is good, sunny and warm, currently 29 degrees. We don't expect any delays and we hope you enjoy your flight."

All pretty customary stuff, I thought.

Then, right at the end of his welcome speech, the pilot announced, "And just to let you know, folks, we have a couple of Hindus down the back. We hope they behave themselves and we would like to wish both a very pleasant flight."

Lee jumped up. "He can't fucking say that, can he?"

"I don't care what he can or cannot say, I'm more concerned with the Hindus at the back."

The plane was silent, and slowly and simultaneously Lee and I turned our heads to look down the back. We saw two "hen do" parties, clearly wondering why everyone was looking at them.

The whole plane roared with laughter, then the pilot came back on, clumsily apologising for his poor pronunciation and trying to be as PC as he could. This just made it funnier, and in seconds the entire flight was in hysterics with laughter. I kept thinking, it's much better than the last flight.

We got to Malaga and met Pearl at Arrivals. The girls were in school and she had Sunny, now a bonnie baby, with her. No cameras this time; not for me or Manchester United FC.

We got to Clive's and I reacquainted myself with Taylor, who was now five. I also met Clive's little boy for the first time. Clive told us that Michael, Stephen O'Driscoll's son, was staying with him too. So, although not pushed for space, he asked would it be okay for Lee and me to share the spare room. Lee and I had never shared a bed, but we knew it wasn't a problem.

As the day went on – most of it spent on the sun roof playing with the kids – Michael came home. He was twenty-five and spent most of his adult life travelling the world and partying. After dinner, Michael said, "Right, boys, where are we going tonight?"

Lee and I were knackered and said we'd rather stay in, but Michael was having none of it.

We got ready for what I thought was going to be a quiet night, maybe go to a couple of local bars. But that's not how it turned out. Lee changed into his black jeans and a black T-shirt with "True Class" written in huge diamante letters on the front.

We walked from the old town towards the seafront. It was after eight but still really warm and, although not in season, it was still quite busy. We had a drink in a couple of bars and ended up in the famous Square. It was buzzing with revellers and we had a great night.

We met up with a few of Michael's friends and went from bar to bar until I'd had enough. Lee was having a ball and had his eye on some girl, so he stayed with Michael, who reassured me he would make sure he got home safe and sound. I said my drunken goodbyes and got a taxi back to Clive's; it was nearly 3am at this stage. I climbed into bed and went to sleep.

At 5.20am I was woken by Michael, who was shaking me gently. "Wake up, John," is all I could hear.

I squinted at the clock and said angrily, "Will you fuck off, Michael? I've only just got to sleep."

Then came the words that would change that trip in its entirety. "Lee's gone missing."

I jumped out of the bed. "What do you mean?"

"He just disappeared," Michael said, panicked and a little bit afraid of my reaction.

"Well, get out there and find him."

I got dressed quickly and realised that not only did Lee not have his mobile with him, but he didn't even know Clive's address let alone his way about the Costa del Sol.

I ran downstairs and Michael was telling Clive about Lee's disappearance. "Get out there and find him," I shouted at Michael, and he ran down the other flight of stairs to the main entrance.

"Calm down, John, you'll burst a vessel," said Clive, with a look of worry on his face.

I had a coffee and collected my thoughts, all the time thinking Lee would walk through the door at any moment. I decided to wait until lunchtime before panicking, and in the meantime I would go looking for him on my own. I walked down to the seafront and all the way up to the Square. It was only 7am but it was starting to get warm and there wasn't a cloud in the sky.

I walked for about an hour then decided I needed a coffee and something to eat, so I went to the first McDonalds I could find. I ordered a breakfast and asked the assistant if they had any newspapers. I sat down with a copy of El Mundo and ate my sausage McMuffin.

Why had I got a Spanish paper? I thought. But then I decided to practise my Spanish, so I started to read. I couldn't believe the headline story; my Spanish wasn't great but it was very clear to me. A gang of Romanian men had been gang raping young men for the past few weeks.

Now Lee was twenty-seven then, but looked about eighteen. No way was this actually happening, and yet it was. This made me even more determined to find him. I walked down to the Square but all the bars were closed. I went into a kebab shop opposite the Square and asked the owner if he had seen Lee. He spoke Arabic – just my luck – and he hadn't a clue what I was on about.

I tried to describe Lee: small, cute, looks eighteen, thin, dark hair and blue eyes. But he was having none of it. Then I remembered his very unique T-shirt.

"True class," I said, as if he was deaf and not foreign, whilst indicating where it was on the shirt.

"Ah, true class." Finally the penny dropped and it turns out Lee had been there only half an hour before. He'd had a cold drink and was asking people where Pearl's pub was. Thank God, I thought; the relief.

I called Pearl and she and Nathan reckoned he'd find his way back. I wasn't too sure, so I decided to keep on looking.

I spent that entire day walking up and down the Costa, in and out of bars, cafes and generally everywhere. It got to 6pm and I started to worry. I knew Lee had very little money on him. I made my way back to Pearl's and decided to wait until it got to 10pm before deciding what to do next. But Pearl and I had an appointment that night at 8pm. We had to meet Wayne's new solicitor, Francisco.

Pearl picked me up from Clive's at 7.45pm and we drove to the local general hospital.

"Why are we going to a hospital, Pearl?" I asked, rather confused.

"He doesn't know the area, so we thought it would be best to meet at a local landmark." Pearl parked the car in a dimly-lit spot and Francisco arrived about ten minutes later.

A bit better than the last crook, I thought; tall, slim, good-looking and, importantly to me, he wore a suit.

Pearl did the introductions and Francisco discussed the case file which he had only just got hold of that very day. All the time I'm thinking, would you hurry up? I still have to find Lee.

Francisco took out the large file and placed it on the bonnet of his car. His English was good, not perfect but better than my Spanish. He explained that there were two alleged murderers and that there was very little evidence to convict Wayne. The only real evidence was that Wayne admitted to being at the scene. He would need more time to examine the file.

Before he left, he asked if we wanted to see the pictures of the crime scene. "No," I said firmly, but I did ask if there were any pictures of Kaiser, Wayne's American Pitbull.

"Yes," he said, and pulled out an A4 photo of a dead Kaiser. He had been shot by the Spanish police. I told Francisco to do his best with the case and we parted.

When we got back into the Jeep, Pearl asked what I wanted to do. "Find Lee," I told her.

At that moment, Wayne rang from the prison. Now my dilemma was whether to go to the police to report Lee missing, or to ask Wayne to call a search amongst his many friends on the Costa.

I took the phone from Pearl and said to Wayne, "Hi, little brother, I need a favour."

"What's up?" he asked.

"Lee's gone missing and he has no mobile or money. He won't have a clue how to find Clive's house."

"Calm down," he said. "I'll call a search on."

"Should I go to the police?" I asked, now at the point of exhaustion.

"No, we'll find him," came the firm reply.

"Ok, thanks," I replied, now at least a little reassured that we would find Lee safe and sound.

"Don't worry, John. See you Friday, love you."

"I love you, too, and thanks, Wayne," I said.

Pearl asked if I had enough energy left to do one more thing before I called it a day. I really couldn't think of doing anything but asked her what she had in mind. She explained that she'd managed to get hold of Juan's address in the mountains. She further explained that he'd been avoiding her calls, so she'd put it out that Wayne's even crazier brother was on the Costa and that I wanted every penny of the money he'd stolen.

I thought, you cannot be serious, but I went along with it. We did need the money after all, so off we drove up the mountains to a very exclusive, small housing complex, surrounded by large fencing. It was 10pm or thereabouts, and we were here to intimidate a bent solicitor in the mountains of Malaga. Could my life get any stranger? And where the fuck was Lee?

Pearl and I looked at the various intercom buttons on the pillar supporting the huge ornate gates at the entrance to the complex. Number 29 was Juan's but, unlike the other residents, he'd removed his name from the little plastic sleeve below the button. We pushed that button a thousand times, but either he wasn't in or he was hiding in his luxury house. We decided to leave it and headed back to Clive's.

On the way I asked if we could go for a drive on the front, just in case Lee was walking about. I don't know where the energy was coming from, but we didn't just drive. Pearl parked up near a hotel and we split up, with me working my way towards the Square and Pearl looking at the opposite end.

We spent the next couple of hours in and out of every shop, cafe, bar, and even brothels, but no way could we find Lee. At one point we decided to have a beer in Molly Malone's in the Square. We sat in the large conservatory-type smoking area where we had a panoramic view of the Square. We just sat there sipping on a beer and watching; we were now totally knackered.

When we finished our beers, I said to Pearl, "Come on then, let's start looking again."

Pearl suggested we walk simultaneously towards the Jeep, with me on one side of the road and her on the other.

"I feel like a pair of undercover coppers," she said.

"Yes, me too," I replied. "Cagney and Lacey," I joked, "and I'm the good-looking blond one."

"What does that make me?" she asked.

"The fat ugly one," I said, and we went off again on our search.

It was useless. Pearl dropped me at Clive's and we arranged to start the hunt for Lee the following morning.

I didn't sleep that night, and after a cold shower I called Pearl. I told her I was going to report Lee missing officially. I'd found his passport in his suitcase and brought it with me to the police station in Benalmadena Old Town.

I walked into the station, Lee's passport in hand, and nervously asked for an English-speaking officer. I hadn't time to practise my Spanish. The officer on the desk went to get an interpreter. Great, I thought, at least they're taking me seriously.

After a few minutes, the interpreter came and brought me into a small room where another Spanish-speaking officer sat at a computer and they proceeded to take my statement. They rang round all the other stations but Lee hadn't been found. They reassured me they would be looking for Lee and advised me to make posters and put them everywhere.

Pearl met me outside the police station and we planned a day of searching and putting up the posters, which we made using a blown-up version of Lee's passport picture and A4 paper. We put them everywhere from Torremolinos to Marbella, and everywhere in between.

As we drove about, we were stopped by many of Wayne's mates in their blacked-out Jeeps and cars.

"Nothing yet," was the general greeting we got, but at least we knew they were looking. The police had told me to keep them informed of any progress and also that they would be sending a helicopter to look should it get dark and there was still no sign of Lee.

The day became night and everyone was exhausted. Then, just as we were giving up, a sighting of Lee was made. Someone had seen him near to Clive's house. We arranged to have the area searched in military style. I wanted every street scoured in a circular fashion from a three mile radius, working our way inwards towards Clive's.

The search was structured and organised but yet again we couldn't find Lee, then I remembered the police and the helicopter. They sent it out at once and we all hoped and prayed that it would find him. Nothing. This led to another sleepless night, which slowly became dawn.

The day was very much like the previous one but with one big difference. The police called and asked me to check the hospitals and, most importantly, the hospital morgues. I discussed this with Pearl and she reminded me that the police said they would do this anyway as a matter of course. So why did we have to do it? we wondered.

I called the policeman back and asked for the interpreter. He explained to me that it was possible Lee was unconscious, or could have amnesia, or in the worst case scenario, he was dead. This was why we had to check personally, so with that grim thought firmly in our minds we spent most of the day visiting the hospitals and morgues. Still no Lee.

Luckily we only had to show his picture at the morgues and didn't actually have to see any bodies. As we were driving to the seafront, Pearl had a call from Nathan.

"Quick, get to the Old Town," he said. There had been another sighting of Lee and this time he was asking for directions to Clive's house.

Pearl drove like the wind to the Irish bar he had been seen at. We were met there by Sasha, Pearl's friend, who had moved there several years ago. Sasha had some further news. Lee was fine, Pearl did the talking and I sat on the kerb in the sweltering heat and cried.

He was fine, that's all I needed to hear. Pearl came to comfort me but I didn't need comfort. I just needed to find Lee. Then I remembered something I should have thought of already. Clive's mate, the radio DJ. Pearl called Clive and thank God, his mate was on air and he put out an urgent appeal for any sightings of Lee, on the hour every hour.

I told the police about this latest sighting and they said they would increase the numbers of coppers searching, and they would concentrate on this area only.

We continued with the search until a heart-stopping text message came. It was Big Steve, Lee's stepdad, and read: "John, it's Steve, ring urgently."

I had to ring Lee's landline number in Manchester. Oh my God, I thought, how do they know he's missing? And what was I going to tell them?

Pearl suggested that maybe it was something else that was "urgent", but that didn't matter, as I explained to Pearl, because whatever it was, I could hardly not mention the small matter of their son being a missing person with Madeleine McCann-style posters of him all over the Costa. Not to mention the three police services looking for him and the poxy radio pleas. Oh no, Pearl, if the urgent thing is something else, I'll just say Lee's fine, lying by the pool!

I needed some time to think so we went for a coffee and then to a local internet shop to make the call.

Big Steve answered the phone and immediately he said, "Have you found him?"

During that conversation it transpired that Lee had called home and left a message that he was lost, and to tell John that he would wait at the Dog Shop. I reassured Steve and Michelle that everything was being done to find him, and I would call them when we did indeed find him.

Wayne called and I told him about the sightings and Lee's call. He said he'd have someone wait at the dog shop, but which one? There were dog groomers all over the place. I told him to cover each one, then I remembered that there was a brand new one near the train station.

I waited at that one for the rest of the day until we again decided to call it a day and try to get some sleep. The police rang before I climbed into bed, asking for an update. No news, I told them. This was now day two, going into day three, and although it was really hot during the day, it became bitterly cold at night. And Lee had only got his True Class T-shirt to keep him warm.

I didn't sleep much and got up the following day, making my way towards the new dog shop. Everyone would have to go through this nightmare yet again.

After a morning and afternoon of the same thing, Nathan called and told me to get back to Clive's, as there had been yet another sighting of Lee. I now had an inkling into what the McCanns must have gone through, although I was lucky as Lee was not a defenceless child.

The search continued and I waited on the little veranda on the first floor of Clive's house, which overlooked the narrow street below. I tried to control my PTSD through breathing and walking up and down on the veranda. Clive and some others came back about 4pm.

I was just about to light a cig when Clive bounded through the French windows leading onto the veranda.

"We've got him."

I fell to my knees and stopped my fall, cutting my palms in the process. My breathing became heavy and laboured and I couldn't speak.

"Take your time, John, just breathe slowly," Clive said, and within minutes I was on my feet again.

"Who found him, Clive?" I asked.

"It was Michael, they're on their way back now."

"Is Lee okay?"

"Yes, John, he's tired and hungry, but he seems to be okay."

Clive went back inside and I lit that cig, then I heard Lee and Michael in the street below, just about to come through the front door. Lee had a McDonald's box in his hand.

I shouted down, "Lee!"

He looked up smiling and said, "Hiya, mate!"

I was fuming. "Get your fucking arse up here now!" I bellowed. Everyone fell silent.

A few minutes later Lee crept onto the veranda. I wanted to kill him for putting us all through this, but instead I hugged him half to death.

He had cuts and bruises, a bad limp in his right leg, and some strange burn mark on his arm, but other than that he was okay. I told him to eat and get a bath, which he did and decided that the story of Lee's disappearance could wait till later. Clive then poured me a very large glass of red wine, and told Michael and me that we should take Lee out to a local bar. Lee said he would like that and so, an hour or so later, we got ourselves ready and walked to the seafront where we sat and listened to Lee telling us what had happened to him.

On the way, Lee went to the internet shop to call his mum to let her and everybody know he was okay. It was now nearly 10pm and dark. As we were chatting, Lee suddenly looked up.

"That's a police helicopter, it must be looking for someone," he said.

"Yes, you," I replied. "You idiot."

We laughed until I suddenly remembered that I was the idiot. I'd forgotten to tell the police that we'd found him. It could wait till morning, I decided, as I was enjoying Lee's tale and our drinks in the warm evening sea air.

It turns out that Lee had left the bar in the Square to have a cig, but was approached by the Civil Guard who grabbed him and slapped him about, apparently accusing him of smashing a car window. In the struggle, he managed to break free from the police and ran. As he ran off, one of the coppers tasered him in the arm, thus explaining that burn mark.

Frightened and sore, he just kept running in the wrong direction. He damaged a ligament in his shin, which explained his limp, and spent the next few days looking for Clive's house. He slept in doorways and couldn't hand himself in to the police for obvious reasons.

I was determined to ensure Lee had at least a few days of rest and relaxation, but we had the small matter of Juan to sort, and Pearl and I were to visit Wayne the following Friday.

The next day Lee and I made our way to the police station. As we got near, I asked Lee to wait at the Burger King while I went to tell the police that we had found him. I didn't want to risk Lee being arrested for resisting arrest that night.

I went in and they again got the interpreter. I sat in another small room and, before I had a chance to say anything, the Spanish-speaking officer said through the interpreter that they had found Lee and that he was locked up in the remand centre.

I couldn't believe what I was hearing. Sure, Lee was outside munching on a Big Breakfast. What was this copper on about? I thanked them and left as quickly as I could.

I sat with Lee, who got me a coffee, and told him what the police had said.

"So, let me get this clear," he said, trying to work it out. "They've arrested some poor fucker who looks like me, and stuck him in the remand centre where we are visiting Wayne tomorrow?"

"Looks like it," I said. And we both burst out laughing. We surely would remember this trip forever.

Pearl picked us up from the beach at four-ish. We spent the day lazing in the sun and really had a nice day. Lee's leg was still sore but it was getting better.

Before we had left Manchester, my good friend Maggie came to the shop with a little gift for me. It was a beautiful little grey teddy bear in a presentation box, a Friendship Bear. That bear had a tiny little, almost unreadable, storybook attached to the box. The story was called, "A Grey Bear with a Blue Nose, The Story of You and Me".

As Lee lay sunbathing, it was my intention to write, but I couldn't think of anything to write.

"Lee, I'm stuck. I can't think of anything to write today," I said.

He replied, "Read that little book Maggie gave you. You must have brought it with you for a reason."

I decided to transcribe that book into my book, wondering all the time: why? Maggie was yet to face her biological father in court and his two brothers. They were to answer to 109 counts of rape against Maggie and her two sisters.

The little story book reads...

"The oldest, smallest house you can imagine was about to be knocked down. All the things that once made the house nice and cosy had been thrown outside and piled up in the garden, from the soft springy bed the owners slept in, to the old wooden floorboards they used to walk on...and even and surely by some mistake, a little brown teddy bear. He was trapped amongst all the other unwanted things and couldn't move.

Then one day, a very, very cold day, something fell from the sky, a little snowflake. It landed on the little teddy bears nose and was followed by many more. He began to get very cold, very cold indeed. More and more snow fell, heavier and heavier. The little bear was now so cold that his nose started turning blue...so cold that his brown fur started turning grey. He was cold, unloved and all alone in the world and felt very, very sad.

Winter finally passed and the weather got warmer. One beautiful spring day, a little girl was playing near the old house, when she spotted the grey bear in the pile of unwanted things. He was like no other bear she had ever seen and she pulled him out from where he was trapped. She dusted him down and lifted him high in the sky to look at him. "A grey teddy bear with a blue nose," she thought, "how strange." The teddy bear wanted to cry, he thought she didn't like him and would throw him back with all the unwanted things. "But he's lovely," she continued and she fell completely in love with him. She ran home as fast as her little legs could carry her, to see if her Grandma could patch him up as a lot of his stuffing had fallen out and he was very much in need of repair. She looked on as her Grandma replaced his stuffing and patched up his holes. His stitches had started showing where the fur had worn away, but the little girl thought he looked perfect.

It was all cosy and warm in the little girl's house and the bear felt cosy and warm in his heart. However his nose was still blue and his fur was grey and they would never return to brown. He was unique among teddy bears.

The little girl gave him a great big hug. She loved him now more than anything else in the world, her little grey/blue nosed...Tatty Teddy.

The relevance of this story to Maggie and me is huge and, I guess, obvious. Just as I finished writing it down, Lee jumped up startled.

"Look, John. I can't fucking believe what I'm seeing."

"What are you looking at?" I said.

"Over there, look."

I couldn't believe it either! An old, grey-haired man, who had been sunbathing all day, had moved his windbreaker in an effort to hide the fact that he was being wanked off by a Thai lady who had offered foot massages for five Euro.

"That's no foot she's massaging," said Lee.

With that we got our stuff together and prepared to meet Pearl, as we were to meet Juan in Torremolinos Old Town. He had agreed to pay us at least five thousand Euro.

Pearl picked us up and we made our way to a little tapas bar where we waited and waited.

"Is this arsehole ever going to turn up?" I asked angrily.

"I think he's giving you the runaround," said Lee.

Pearl and I decided to call him one more time. Would he answer the phone this time? No, he was taking the piss and we decided to call it a day.

We went back to Clive's and decided to have a night out; a proper night out. We got ready at Clive's and headed for the Square. Pearl said she'd meet us with some other friends at a mixed bar on the main strip.

Lee wasn't very comfortable in gay bars as he got a lot of unwanted attention from men, but he was happy enough to go to this bar. I'd made sure he had Clive's address on him this time, and enough money.

The bar was buzzing, with lots of great dance music at full blast and it certainly was a mixed crowd. We managed to get a table with four stools, as Michael had joined us. We drank, danced and did that loud bar chatting thing of actually shouting in an effort to hear each other.

I felt really relaxed that night. I wasn't the raped man; yet again, I was John, enjoying a night on the Costa del Sol with friends and family.

Just before we left to go to Molly Malone's, a gay couple started hitting on Lee.

"I wish those two would fuck off," he shouted.

I leaned forward and shouted back, "Kiss me."

"What? Kiss you?" came the surprised reply.

"Yes, just kiss me." And he did. "They'll fuck off now, Lee, you watch."

And fuck off they did.

We spent the rest of the night having a ball in Molly Malone's and danced the night away. I knew we couldn't go too mad as tomorrow was another important day; it was another visit to the prison to see Wayne.

We had a great night, however, and Lee didn't even get lost. When we got back to Clive's at stupid o'clock – so much for not going mad then – Lee and I decided to sit on the sun roof and gaze at the stars. It was getting cold so I got us some blankets.

Lee managed to fix the broken radio in our room, so we had music too. He rolled a joint and I got the wine. We'd stopped at a store that day and I'd bought what I thought was a really delicate white wine; made in the mountains of Malaga, it said on the label. Or at least, I thought it did. We made ourselves comfy with Lee sitting on the love swing, and me wrapped up all snug next to him. Lee smoked his joint, pure Moroccan gold, and I poured the wine.

I took a mouthful of wine and nearly froze. "What the fuck?"

"What's up?" asked Lee.

"This is like rocket fuel!"

Lee burst out laughing, and at exactly that moment *Rocket Man* by Elton John came on the radio. We laughed so hard it hurt, but I finished the bottle of rocket fuel and Lee got nicely stoned. I went to bed a lot worse for wear and Lee said he wanted to stay up a bit longer.

The following morning I woke Lee, shaking his shoulder gently.

"Fuck off, will you? My leg's in bits!"

"What's up?" I said.

"I fell through the poxy swing," came the reply. And we started that day as we had finished the last, laughing.

Pearl picked us up for our visit to Wayne and we got to the prison at 5pm. It was really hot that day, particularly hot, and, combined with massive hangovers, none of us was in good spirits.

Lee was looking forward to finally meeting Wayne but they wouldn't allow him in as he wasn't family. It was meant to be a "special" visit, not one where glass separated us but in a room where we could actually hug. Wayne messed up the visit by relying on Francisco to organise it; it was his responsibility not his solicitors, and therefore the visit would have to be a "normal" one.

Pearl and I got through the now familiar mayhem and finally to the allocated phone booth and waited for Wayne while Lee stayed in the Jeep.

Out Wayne hobbled, still on crutches, and he sat down. I felt much more comfortable than on the previous visit, it didn't matter that there were potential rapists on the other side of the glass. Sure, Wayne was there too and he wouldn't let anyone hurt me, crutches or not.

We started our chat. How was Dad, was Wayne's first question. I'd made sure he was fully informed of Dad's progress, but I must admit to overdoing the "he's fine" line, when we all knew Dad was seriously ill.

I was just about to ask him how his leg was doing when he stopped me in my tracks and said, "What's that on your face?"

Shit, I thought. There was a momentary pause until Pearl interrupted the silence and said, without thinking, "John's writing a book."

Oh my God, I thought. So now I have to explain the trauma cyst on my face from the repeated punches during the rape, and I had to explain my book. Wayne had no clue that I'd been raped, let alone was writing a book about it.

Pearl's mistake worked.

"What are you writing a book about? Sure, what's happened in your life to write about?"

Thank God, I thought. I don't have to tell him what caused the lump on my right cheekbone which reminded me every time I caught a glimpse of myself, of what caused it.

"My book's about life, little brother. My life, yours and even Dad's," I explained.

"Oh," he said, "will it be a movie one day?"

"I don't know, maybe one day," I replied. "Who would you like to play you?"

"Brad Pitt," came the prompt reply.

"That role's already taken," I said, flicking my long hair over my shoulder and flexing my muscles. "He's playing me."

We all laughed and enjoyed the rest of the short, but vitally important, visit.

The time up bell rang and I left the booth so that Pearl could say her personal goodbye, then I went back in and stared into his eyes, now – as expected – filled with tears. I placed my palm on the glass and he did the same.

He mouthed the words, "Are you sure nothing bad's happened?"

I imagined hearing his voice, in his strong Dublin brogue.

"I'm sure, little brother," I mouthed back, tears streaming down my face and wanting to choke on my own lies.

He was having none of it. "I want to know what's happened. We never lie to each other!"

I couldn't hear him, but he was shouting loud and I couldn't answer him. The guard came and dragged him to the door.

Just before he went through the doorway, he mouthed angrily, "I know something's happened. We're the Irish Kray twins, for fuck's sake. We don't lie to each other."

Pearl came through and did what Clive had done. I wasn't on my knees but I was close. I was holding myself up with my wrists placed heavily on the shelf with that poxy hole, the only method of communicating with my baby brother.

"Come on, John" she said, with her arm resting gently on my shoulder. "He'll be okay," she said.

I left that visit with one thing on my mind. How was I going to tell him? I had no choice other than to tell him before he found out from somebody else.

This was to be our last day on this trip, and Lee and I spent the day buying little pressies to take home to Manchester. We walked about Torremolinos, browsing through the souvenir shops. I bought some of the usual tack, tea towels, fridge magnets and such. Lee bought his mum a bottle of Bacardi with matching glasses in a presentation box.

He had a new dilemma, what to buy for his Auntie Sharon. Sharon is autistic and lives with Lee's family, but what to buy her was a particularly difficult task. In the end he bought a box of sweets which he knew she would like.

We then went onto the beach for the last time, we had Burger King for lunch and then Lee bought one more gift for his brother, Chris. A guy was selling hand-drawn charcoal portraits on the seafront and Lee haggled with him, getting a picture of TuPac for fifteen, and not the asking price of twenty Euro.

Pearl and Nathan took us to the airport and we were a bit cautious checking in, as there was still the possibility that Lee was wanted. It was fine though, and we had an uneventful trip back to Manchester.

Big Steve picked us up from the airport and Lee and I told him all about our adventures in Malaga. Then I collected Indie from Linda and Malley's, and got home quite late that evening.

≈ 13 ≈

Intimate Disclosure

I was woken at 3am by the mobile; it was Wayne, calling from his cell. I poured a glass of wine and prepared myself for that call. I didn't answer the phone at first as I knew what was coming. I called his mobile, this was the third one he had had smuggled into the prison.

"Hiya, little brother, can't you sleep?"

"Fuck sleep, tell me what's wrong?"

I had kept it from him for so long and I knew this was the moment I was going to have to tell Wayne that I'd been raped, but I couldn't get the words out. I told him to make himself comfortable and that I'd call him back.

I went to find "My Journey to Justice?", which at that stage was twenty-or-so handwritten pages in a hard-backed diary. I called Wayne.

"What's all this 'get comfy' business? Just tell me what's wrong," he said angrily.

"Calm down," I told him. "Do you remember when we were kids and you'd wake in the night looking for a bedtime story?"

"Yeah," he said, becoming curious.

"Well, sit down, Wayne, I'm going to read you a bedtime story now," I said, holding back the tears. And I started to read my book.

When I got to the part "when the monster raped me", there was silence. More silence. Then Wayne screamed like I have never heard a man scream. At that point I regretted telling him, but everybody knew and I obviously couldn't tell him during our visits, so I knew deep down I had done the right thing.

His screams got louder and deeper; he was angry and I recognised this sound, the sound of Wayne's anger. He was thrashing his room, banging and kicking things, and I was worried he would get into trouble, so I shouted down the phone to him, like I would if he was being naughty as a kid.

"Sit down now!" I yelled, with every bit of energy I had. There was silence again.

"Wayne!" I shouted. "Pick up the phone, please pick up the phone." I could hear him slump against the cell wall and, crying, fall to the ground. He was sobbing as he put the phone to his ear.

"When?" he said, trying to hold it together.

"The twenty-fifth of August, 2010, at 6.31am," I said.

"How do you remember the time?" he asked, a little bit more gathered in his thoughts.

"It's a date and time I will never forget. Wayne, are you calm now?" I replied.

"Yes," came the reply.

I told him to forget any thoughts of revenge and to concentrate on getting himself out of there and, not least to remember that we had a father, a good dad, who was ill and needed us both.

"What prison is he in?" came the reply.

A waste of time trying to calm him, was my first thought, but then I had no idea what prison the monster was in. So I told him in a very matter of fact way that I had no idea.

"How long did he get?" was the next question.

This was like court all over again, but how my brother in prison had suddenly become a barrister – the defence or prosecution – in this conversation, I couldn't fathom. I wasn't having this again, so I started to shout again.

"Shut the fuck up, now!"

There was further silence at his end, then a distant sob. I asked him to pick up the phone in as gentle a manner as I could, then waited as my baby brother, who was trying to deal with this terrible news as best he could, lifted the phone.

After what seemed like an eternity, he said, "I love you, John."

I held back the tears and clawed at the air; my palm was empty but he was there. "I love you too, baby brother."

"I have to go, they're coming. I'll get him, promise," came the panicked reply and he was gone.

I spent the rest of that night writing, not about what had just happened, but writing down words which I thought could describe my brother best.

If I was to paint a picture of him here in these pages then I needed to understand my view of him and my understanding of our relationship. I tried to overcome yet more tears whilst writing, and tried in vain to get some sleep.

Some of the words I wrote in my own personal brainstorming session were: strong, proud, adventurous, loving, funny, rebellious, intelligent, father, brother and defender. When I looked at these words, and there were many more, I thought, who is this I'm describing: Wayne or Dad? I concluded, both.

.

≈ 14 ≈

The Great Plumbob

Third of July, 2012, 7.08am.

I was lying in bed with Matthew, the new man in my life. Yes, Matthew. You'd think I'd have learned from the last Matthew, but I was really looking forward to our day together. We planned to go to Heaton Park with Jaya and Indie.

My mobile rang; it was Dean Adam. Half-asleep, I answered it. I knew by his crying what had happened, even though he couldn't speak. Dad, Joe, the great Plumbob, was dead.

Just before I had gone to bed the night before, I had sent Wayne a text: "Dad sent for the kids today, spoke to Holly earlier and she really enjoyed seeing her granddad."

I sorted the dogs out, packed as best I could, and drove around to Liam's. I didn't need to tell him; he just knew at his first glance at my face. I told Liam I would be back in an hour to collect him but I had to drop Matthew at his flat in Stockport.

I collected Liam an hour or so later and we headed over to Withington to collect Linda and Malley. On the way, the mobile rang. It was Wayne. I stopped the car and answered the phone.

We cried, neither of us speaking a word until he said, sobbing, "Look after Mum."

"I will, Wayne, promise. Can you write a few words down?"

"I can't write," he said.

"Just write anything. Do you want me to read it at the funeral?"

"Yes, okay then, I'll write something," he said. And before I hung up, he said, "I love you, John."

And I told him that I love him.

I drove to Holyhead with Uncle Liam in the passenger seat and Linda and Malley in the back. I tried not to crash the car through my tears. The awkward silences were not that awkward, as we were all in the same boat. Linda and I had lost our father, Liam his baby brother, and Malley his father-in-law; most importantly, we had all lost a friend, a true friend.

When we got to the house – the full-to-bursting house; our house and our home – Mum embraced us all individually. We all cried, everyone was sobbing or trying to control their tears. Mum's brother, Tommy, and Auntie Bridie sat on the couch. Bridie said, as she hugged me, that it was the best thing; he was no longer in pain.

Best for who? I thought. Not best for his wife and kids, but she was right, he was no longer in physical or emotional pain, he was no longer frightened. Not frightened for himself, as he was brave, but frightened of what he was leaving behind.

The days, Monday, Tuesday, whatever, came and went. They neither seemed to go quickly nor slowly. The days, this past week, are a blur.

Jake and I drove to Newlands Cross Cemetery and Jessie met us there. The idea was to choose a plot for Dad. Mum led the way with the man from the office – a nice man; "honest", Uncle Liam described him as. We walked down the neatly and immaculately kept cemetery to Dad's grave. It had an AstroTurf cover with planks of wood as a "lid".

There were lots of trees, but none that would affect Dad's love of the sun. In this eleven-year-old cemetery, this well-groomed modern cemetery, the loved ones in those graves got the same amount of sun, hail, rain or snow; they were all equal.

We drove home, down the Naas Road. Mum said that Linda had spotted Uncle Shay and Auntie Phyllis's grave. Fucking hell, we all thought, none of us knew she was dead.

When we got home, Mum had a call from the undertaker, Massey's. She panicked. Dad was coming home an hour early. Not the planned 3.30pm, but now 2.30pm. There was so much to do.

I drove to the Bank of Ireland with Linda, Malley and Tash. On the way, we stopped at the photo restoration shop, and Tash chose the most beautiful photo of Dad, on holiday in Lanzarote. The lady in the shop used her computer to "crop out" Linda and Mum.

Tash paid the thirty Euro – a bargain, we all agreed. The frame would match the coffin and that photo was perfect; it caught his character and, of course, he would be wearing a D&G T-shirt. We changed our money and got back home at 2.15pm.

Dad came home. The room, his room, was ready, or at least we thought it was. We'd scrubbed it, moved out the big armchair and Dad's TV. Everyone thought he looked perfect; I thought he looked plastic, but it was the great Plumbob nonetheless. Joe, my dad, was home.

There had been lots of discussions amongst us all as to where to position his coffin, but the guys from Massey's said the best place was in the bay window. We could regulate the temperature using the windows and a couple of fans that friends had brought. I'd taken his navy blue suit, with his favourite pink shirt and blue and pink tie, to Massey's the previous day. He looked good, but his hair was brushed back. Dad would be fuming; he always brought his hair forward and sometimes he liked a side parting. Everyone commented on his hair, but could we use gel or mousse? Nobody knew.

"He looks so peaceful."

"God, he looks twenty years younger."

"Not a line on his face."

"They have done a great job."

"Ah, sure, they really look after them at Massey's."

All of these comments, words of comfort, in my head were silence breakers, words to fill the void. But who was there to fill the eternal void left by Dad?

The days came and went; visitors, more and more visitors, phone calls, flowers, text messages and emails. My God, I thought, at this rate we'll be getting poxy smoke signals and planes carrying banners. But, hey, Dad was a popular man, loved the world over.

What was most important, of prime importance to my father, was his family. My family; Mum and Dad's kids, their grandchildren and great-grandchildren. The Lennons are a big clan and Dad's immediate and extended clan meant everything to him.

Who was coming from his brothers and sisters would have been most important to Dad. I knew Josie, Kevin, Maggie, Jenny, Big and Young Ron and Barbara would be there, but who else? We'll see, I thought, because there was that much to think about.

I said to whoever was listening, "If they get here, they get here!"

Liam and I knew Uncle John would be there, come rain, hail or snow. He'd had his own cancer operation the Friday before Dad died; skin cancer on his back. The operation had been successful but he'd never carry the coffin, neither could my big brother, Paul, with his heart condition. But they were there, we all were.

169

The day came, my father's wake. I'd made him cups of
tea every morning that week, wondering would he think I'd
gone mad. I made that tea as he would have liked it, strong
with one sugar. I joked with Mum about how Dad would
make his tea; he'd annoy us all by stirring it so hard it sounded
like a crime scene, but we all wanted to see the pile of used
teabags that would pile up on the sink.

That pile of teabags would be there for days as Mum
would refuse to put them in the bin. Today I didn't make Dad
his cup of tea, I poured him a whiskey, Bells, I think it was.
Whatever the brand, Dad had a dram, his favourite drink. We
had a wake, a traditional Irish wake. Dad would have loved it.

We waited patiently for the priest. He'd said on Tuesday
after prayers that he'd be there for 7pm. I was trying to look
after everyone, getting them drinks and passing round the
beautiful platters of sandwiches that Rowie, Tasha's friend,
had made. The driveway was full of friends and family, every
room in our home was full to bursting – getting to the loo
became a real issue.

I paced up and down, no priest. 7.10pm, still no priest. I
looked up and down Dolphin Road. There are yellow lines
forbidding any cars from parking after 6pm. The road was full
of parked cars. Would the police have the guts to disturb
Dad's wake? Let them fucking try, I thought.

7.15 then 7.20, and still no priest. Then someone asked
me to ask Cousin Breena to lead a decade of the rosary.

"I couldn't say a fucking Our Father," she said.

Jesus Christ, I thought, what were we going to do? 7.25
and panic over; the priest finally arrived. I was fuming.

As he casually walked up the drive, I said to him in no
uncertain terms, "Father, you're late."

He replied, as cool as a cucumber, "Sure, you young ones
are always in such a hurry these days."

I was flabbergasted, speechless, but in my head I thought, read those poxy prayers or I'll put you in that canal. That's what Dad would have done.

The wake ended with me in bed at 3am-ish, I think. I woke the following day at 7am, the day of Dad's funeral. I made him his cup of tea and checked his make-up and his hair. Everything was fine. He had his rosary beads in his clasped hands, and all the things we had placed in his coffin were still neatly placed, despite all the visitors he'd had.

Faith and Ellie May had put in little notes, both in English and Spanish; Roy and Scott put medals in that they'd won recently for running and hurling; Jessie had placed a tiny little guardian angel in a little gift bag, and everyone made a contribution. There was Dad's measuring tape, his mobile phone and, of course, his plumb line.

I put Indie's Endal medal in his hand; Indie's award for bravery. Dad deserved that medal, so in it went.

The service was to be held about a mile down the road at Dolphin's Barn Church at noon. My suit was ready, although I had to buy some new black pants from Penny's as my original ones had faded slightly. I bought a new white shirt and a two-toned, black silk tie. The whole lot came to twenty-two Euro, so I treated myself to a three Euro pair of black and silver sunglasses.

Everyone started to arrive. Where the hell were we going to put them? Again, just like yesterday, hordes of people were crammed into our home. People had slept wherever they could find a relatively comfy spot, and getting ready for the funeral had been bedlam.

I'd managed to get to bed before everyone else and even managed to get a shower and shave in the morning. When ready, I ran to the local garage for milk and yet more bread. Dawn came with me as she had to go to the post office. On the way out of the garage, I spotted Dawn in the street embracing two men. They had their backs to me but as I walked over to them I realised it was Eddie, Dad's nephew, and Stevie, his brother. They walked over to me and Eddie gave me the biggest hug. I sobbed in his arms. That was the first time I'd "let go" as they call it; the first time in public anyway.

We went back home and everyone gave them the biggest welcome. The big clean-up was well underway. Everyone helped – kids, grandkids, in-laws, everyone. The house, front and back gardens looked great and, despite our hangovers, we did it.

The hearse was to arrive at 11.45am. The driveway was full of flowers. There were all kinds of bouquets and arrangements but the biggest and boldest were "Dad", "Granddad", "Joe", and a huge yellow, "Plumbob".

I handed out single yellow roses with blank cards to my sisters and Paul. We all wrote something private, a little message to Dad. Mine read, "I love you, Dad, but I could kill you for nothing."

Dad used to jokingly shake his fist at us as kids, and later at the grand and great-grandkids and say, "I'll kill you for nothing." It always made us smile.

Mum asked me to write Wayne's card as he had been refused bail the previous week, so obviously wasn't there. What would I write? I thought. Do I write in Spanish or English? Then I thought, fuck this, I'll ring him. His phone was dead, or he'd turned it off, or the screws were about. Whatever, he didn't answer so I went upstairs and sat on Dad's bed and wrote Wayne's card: "I love you, Dad, your number one son, Wayne x."

It got to 10.30 and we all waited patiently for the hearse. It came early; too early, I thought. It was only 11am.

Mum wanted us to carry the coffin to the church. The undertaker had said earlier in the week that it would depend on the weather. The weather that week had been beautiful almost tropical, but today it was pissing down buckets, all day.

172

The priest said at the service that if it rained on the day a person was being buried, it meant the person was happy. What a load of shite, I thought at the time.

Josie, Ron and the gang had arrived at 7.30 that morning. I heard them when I was getting ready. As I was dressing, I hoped and prayed that Josie had brought the photo of Nicky, Dad's brother who had died when Dad was only a child. Nicky died of meningitis when he was only seven years old.

When Dad had been in intensive care, he asked me to try to find a picture of Nicky. I made sure the one and only photo of him in existence was found. Aunt Maggie had "borrowed" it from Gran and, thank God, she had kept it safe all these years. Josie had brought the photo and she gave it to me to place it in with Dad.

What a scrawny kid, I thought. And what had he got on? His shorts looked like a skirt, but at least he had shoes on as most of the kids didn't in those days. I gave the photo back to Josie and asked her to place it in with Dad; it seemed more appropriate somehow.

Everyone anticipated the moment, the moment we would place the lid on my dad's coffin. Uncle Kevin acted like a doorman at the front door and I spoke to the undertaker.

"I'm afraid we'll have to use the hearse, the weather's too bad," he explained to me.

"My mother wants him to be carried, and we will carry him – rain or not," I told him,

"OK, John, no problem. Just be careful," he said, backing off.

"Of course we will be careful," I said. "We're carrying precious cargo, not a bag of spuds."

The moment came to say our final goodbye. Dad was going to Church. "I'll kill you all for nothing," he would have said, being – like me – a true atheist.

Before Dad's coffin was closed, we all gathered round for a final decade of the rosary. Mum led the prayers. Being an atheist, I wasn't thinking so much about Dad's soul but more about what number "Hail Mary" we were at. I counted nine but Mum looked at me as if to say, is that ten? I nodded with a very serious face.

The prayers finished and Mum embraced Dad. She sobbed and sobbed over Dad's body. I'm not too sure who kissed him goodbye next, but it came to my turn. I was all the time watching Mum. She'd said to Dad, "I'll be joining you soon."

"Not too bleeding soon," I said, wondering at the time if she'd noticed that I'd said "bleeding". She hadn't.

I clasped Dad's hand as I kissed him on his forehead, somehow his hair or make-up didn't matter. I could feel Uncle Liam's rosary beads in his hands. I didn't cry but pushed the pain deep, deep inside me, because I knew what I and the others had to do. I don't know how long it took for everyone in the house to say goodbye but it seemed like an eternity.

The men got in place and, on instruction from the undertaker, we lifted Dad onto our shoulders. I led the way with Paul, my brother-in-law by my side. Paul grasped my shoulder and I his, and I'm sure he was thinking the same as me. What the fuck had Plumbob got in his coffin – lead weights? It was heavy, really heavy, or maybe I was tired, drained emotionally and physically, but that would have to wait. My dad was going to church for the last time.

"Left foot first," the undertaker said, as we started on the journey.

Behind Paul and me were Malley, Kevin, Dean Adam and Nathan. I couldn't move my feet properly. Was it because the shoes I was wearing had a funny-shaped sole? I'd worn these shoes for many sombre occasions – the monster's trial, Brian and Bettina's funerals, Kelly's monster's trial and now for my father's funeral. Best get some new shoes when I get home, I kept thinking, trying all the time not to break down. Dad would be proud of me.

The funeral director walked ahead of the huge entourage. He had a top hat on and walked with an ornate walking stick. We walked slowly. People lined the streets and held their heads low. Maggie had said to me, if I couldn't carry Dad then she would take over. At the time I thought, you weigh five stone wet through and you're wearing six inch heels.

As we got to the bridge, I had to stop. My PTSD was about to kick in and I wasn't going to allow it to, not today. Everybody kept saying, "Are you okay?"

Paul Kelly shouted, "Of course he's not okay, would you all stop asking."

As the tears took over, I let go and to everyone's surprise, including mine, Maggie took over. She carried Plumbob in six inch heels. I walked about ten steps in front of the entourage. Little hands suddenly and gently slipped inside mine – it was Abbey, Tina's daughter, and Ellie May. They walked with me.

The roads were cordoned off and we led the way – me sobbing uncontrollably and two beautiful angels supporting me. We went left at the lights and slowly made our way over Dolphin's Barn Bridge. We went past Dad's pub, Freehills, and it seemed like the whole of South Dublin had come out to line the streets. As we got closer to the church, I spotted what I thought was an unmarked police car with plain clothes coppers. But why where they there? Surely they knew Wayne was locked up in Malaga. Maybe I got it wrong, and that car left almost as soon as I'd seen it.

We got to the church entrance and Abbey, Ellie and I waited to one side for Dad to be brought in. When he did, we walked slowly behind him, followed by what turned out to be over five hundred people. When we got seated in the front row, Paul sat on the left, next to Dad.

The funeral singer had nearly completed her first song, "*He ain't heavy, he's my brother*". Next to Paul sat Mum, followed by Linda, Michelle, me and Tash.

In what seemed like a microsecond, the priest was nodding at me to come and do my reading, the first reading of the service. As I read, quite clearly and calmly, I didn't see or hear the words. I didn't see any of the huge congregation in the packed church, I just read those words. They meant nothing to me. I just read them whilst trying to control my emotions.

When I finished, I walked over and sat beside Dean Adam. He put his arm around me and I sobbed like a baby. Dean was the next to do a reading. He got up and started his reading and almost got through it, but broke down halfway through. I was just about to go to him, but Linda got there first and she supported him as he completed his reading.

I re-took my seat in the front row, sitting between Michelle and Tash. The funeral singer, who had a beautiful voice, was a bit too enthusiastic. Every time the priest was about to start an important part of the service, she would unexpectedly burst into song. Michelle thought this was hilarious and she started laughing uncontrollably, then I started. Just as we were composing ourselves and hoping that nobody had noticed, she'd do it again and again.

At least she had her mane of blonde hair to hide under; I'd had mine cut short and couldn't hide. Then I thought, Dad would have loved it. The priest wasn't too impressed though.

The kids brought the offerings to be placed in the coffin, but somehow the signed boxing glove from Paddy Dingle, our family friend, wasn't placed in with Dad. The next to do a reading was Pearl, then Natasha. Scott, Roy, Jake and Lorenzo did readings too. Dad would have been very impressed.

Then, the big one. Wayne had written a few words which Pearl had originally planned to read. When Wayne called me on my way over, I promised that I'd read his words. Pearl said she would prefer that too. During the week, however, it became clear that Megan wanted to read her father's words at her grandfather's funeral, but everyone worried she wouldn't be strong enough.

When it came time for Megan to do her "reading", she asked me to go with her, right at the last minute. I stood behind Megan in the pulpit, resting my hands on her shoulders. She was trembling all over, but together we did it. She read her father's words and I was there to take over if necessary, but she did it. Wayne's words to his father were:

"I don't know where to start, it hurts so much to say goodbye to your hero. But at least I know he's in a better place now and any time I need him, he's standing right beside me, ready to take on anything with me. And as I walk through the valley of the shadow of death, I shall fear no evil because I know you are with me and you have a lump hammer under your coat. So say goodbye to a good guy, the great Plumbob, the best Da in the World. Hasta La Vista, y te amo siempre. Thank you everyone for coming and Ma, don't worry, what doesn't break me makes me stronger. Love, your number one son.

Everyone cried and laughed at the "lump hammer" joke and Megan and I took our seats to a huge round of applause. All the kids did a reading. Scott, Roy, Jake, Lorenzo, Jessie contributed in some way to the service.

Dawn was the next person to speak; she looked like a sexy schoolteacher up there with her glasses and sombre suit. She'd asked me to check her speech beforehand, which I had. It was perfect but she'd forgotten to mention the great-grandkids, but she corrected this before reading it. She thanked everyone and talked about her father, his strength and compassion, and most importantly his love for his family.

When we got to the cemetery in the beautiful funeral cars – not sure what make they were – it was still raining. It seemed most people had got there before us. I could see Brian and Gavin in their fine suits.

It was time to carry Dad again. The cars got as close to plot K49 as they could. This time it was Malley by my side. We walked slowly, left foot forward, in the pouring rain, and finally we got there. The gravediggers lowered Dad's coffin carefully into the grave and everyone waited for the priest to start his sermon.

As he was speaking, Mum's friend, a lady in her eighties, held her umbrella over the priest's head. She was bent over in the pouring rain but she wanted to keep him dry. The only problem was, he couldn't see a bleeding thing. I giggled inside. I clung to Megan, hugged her tight, and Wayne listened to all the goings on in his cell. Thank God for mobile phones, I thought.

After all the carefully chosen songs – the most important being "*Old Man River*" by Al Jolson, Dad's favourite – the final song was played as we placed the yellow roses on dad's coffin. "*My Way*" by Old Blue Eyes.

One thing was strange, I thought at the time. Going through my mind was the last time Dad had made me and others laugh. He had just come round from his nine hour operation. I, like the others, had rushed home as the doctors told Dad he might not make it through the op. We could not believe his bravery that day, but he had no need to prove how brave he was. He listened to himself and took his own advice, despite what the doctors told him. We waited around his bed and he woke up, still high on morphine, but he scanned that room and knew we were all there. Mum, Linda, Natasha and I waited with baited breath for his first words.

When he moaned that we didn't have to spend money coming all the way from Manchester, we experienced a feeling of massive relief; a shared feeling.

After a while, he said to me, "Son, I believe you're going to London next week."

"Yes, Dad, that's right," I replied.

"You going for a holiday?" he asked.

"Yes, Dad, that's right and Indie's in a dog show in Earls Court."

"Ah, that's great," he said. "When you get there, could you look someone up for me, please?" he asked.

Dad went on to tell a tale, a joke to make us smile. Or was it, I wondered at the time, the morphine talking? Dad said that his friend, Wobbly Willie, lived in Camden Town and that I should try to find him and have a drink with him. I asked Dad why he was called Wobbly Willie. He explained that Wobbly Willie was a thalidomide victim who had managed to get through to his seventies with only one wobbly arm and no legs.

Dad explained that the last time he had seen him, a couple of years ago, they had gone for a few drinks in Camden Town. Dad met him in the pub and lifted him from his electric wheelchair and sat him on a stool at the bar. Then, without warning, Wobbly Willie punched Dad in the head with his "good" arm.

"Why did he do that, Dad?" I asked, as surprised as the others.

"He said I stood on his toe," came the reply. He truly did have the best sense of humour in the most unexpected of situations.

The white doves were released and my final gesture to my father was to throw a yellow rose onto his coffin. Goodbye, Dad, my dearly loved dad, and missed with every breath I take.

≈ 15 ≈

The Summing Up

When I got home to Manchester, I spent the rest of the week reading the kind words and various verses on the cards and gifts that people had given to me.

I took the week off work and one night, not too sure which, I decided to write to Wayne. That letter reads:

Hi Little Brother,

I really hope you are doing okay, and by the sounds of it you are. Just got back from London, Dawn had Indie for the past two weeks so Lee and I went to pick her up. We had a night in the Black Cap, the gay bar in Camden. I copped off with a black guy, he had a really weird bottom lip. Lee said he looks like Chicken George from the cartoon. We were pissed as farts but a good night was had by all.

Last time we were there, Indie got an award at the London pet show for her role in trying to defend me during the rape. Of course she was only 26 weeks old then, but she did her best. She won a six month supply of really expensive dog food, a medal and the dog version of that picture "Scream". I put her medal in with Dad in the coffin, thought he deserved it more.

Life is strange without Dad, it must be for you too. Everyone has reacted to his sad passing quite differently but, hey, we all grieve in our own way. The funeral was beautiful, he would have been really, really proud and we should all be proud of our individual contributions. Your reading was perfect, not a dry eye in the house and everyone laughed out loud when Megan read the funny bit about the lump hammer. Megan did really well, she was a bit shaky but I stood behind her and held onto her.

I've been busy with lots of stuff. I've co-written a song which the BBC are giving us a studio to record, it's called "No Means No" and is for charity, and Rechelle, Maggie Smith's daughter, is singing it, plus Lee doing a bit of rap.

I'm still being filmed for the Panorama special on victims of rape and the final interview is next Monday in the Gay Village. I'll be talking about sentences and the leniency of them in the UK.

The shop is doing okay, still get quiet days but that's just how the recession has affected the economy. No fucker has any money these days.

I don't want to rabbit on about shit like the economy when really all I want to do is get you out of there and back where you belong with your family and friends. Corrie's on now, gonna watch it and start writing again.

All I can think about is Wednesday, your big day, and I have no clue whether you will be standing in front of that Judge with Francisco or not.

It's Wednesday now, when I found out you didn't know about the hearing on Wednesday, I was fuming. I've been in touch with Francisco and Pearl and she said Nathan's going to give him a piece of our minds. I'm in work now, Lee is on his way, he asks about you all the time, as do all the people in my life, my very complicated life.

The book is a work in progress, I have a publisher now and any chance I get, I send off some more of it typed up. It's been hard fucking work but I think it's a bloody good read, even if I do say so myself.

I'm also volunteering for Survivors Manchester, the charity that helped me. We are putting together a self-help guide for male victims of rape and childhood abuse.

Well, Bro, as I'm typing this clock is ticking towards 3pm and I hope we all have some good news on your case. I'll get these dogs done and write a bit more later. Just to give you an idea of my day at work, Lee and I are having a really busy day, the weather's good you see, and it's the rain that stops people bringing the dogs for grooming.

Today we've had two French Bulldogs, a staff cross, a Lhasa Apsho, a 15-year-old Shepherd, a Shih Tzu and a Jack Russell. The Bulldogs have just had a fight, even though, as Lee just said, they live together. Lee's just cut his hand, you think his bleeding head had been chopped off, for God's sake. It's a scratch but he ran to the first aid kit like a chicken through Cambodia in the 80s.

It's 4 o'clock, Linda's just rang to see have I heard from Francisco or Pearl. Nothing yet, I told her, we are all getting used to this waiting business when it comes to you!

It's now Thursday, Francisco rang at 4.17pm yesterday, and I've been trying to get hold of you all night. Hopefully I will be able to tell you the brilliant news before you get this letter. Well, here goes, you are no longer facing a murder charge, the Judge has accepted that you were involved but you are to be charged with assault with a maximum sentence of 6 years.

Everyone is over the moon. I nearly went into an episode of Post Traumatic Stress Disorder but Lee calmed me down. The other phone call I have been expecting all week, and am sitting here now still waiting for, is from the probation service. You see, the monster is due to be released any day now and all restrictions on his movements will be lifted, apart from the 10 years on the Sex Offenders' Register, but don't worry, I am dealing with this and will cope fine.

I need to tell you something funny that happened today. A customer came into the shop to pick up his two Cavaliers; it was closing time and Lee and I just wanted to get home. I'd left the 'Dogs Today' article open on the counter. Anthony, the customer, started reading it and I tried to stop him.

"Now, don't be shocked," I said.

"Nothing shocks me these days," he replied, and continued reading.

Lee and I swept up and then Anthony put his hands on his head, took a step back and said, "Oh my God, John, what the fuck?"

I told him that he would be shocked, and reassured him I was doing just fine. As he read on, he asked how long the monster got and I told him. He then asked how long the trial was and I told him it went on for weeks.

He then asked, rather confused, "Why so long?"
I told him it was because there were that many witnesses.
"How many witnesses were there, John?" he asked, now baffled. I told him there were dozens of witnesses.
"What?" he shouted. "Dozens of witnesses, and nobody did a fucking thing?" I thought you'd like that, Bro.
Well, little brother, I best sign off now and get on with my job. Let's hope you are out of that place soon, real soon, and we can get all of our lives back to normal; whatever normal is. I love and miss you dearly.

Te amo siempre, su hermano, Juan.

Writing this book has made me realise many things about myself, and life in general. I suppose, on reflection, that my book is predominantly about surviving rape and my near-death experience.

On reading it back to myself, I realise that it is mainly about three people – me, Wayne, and our dear father.

I sincerely hope that it inspires someone to report rape and to have the courage to see their abuser put away.

My brother has endured two years on remand without trial and the Judge, in her supreme wisdom, has now granted another two years remand. This means an innocent man is being held in that place with no idea what his fate will be. However, my family and I have had enough and have enlisted the help of the Irish Embassy in Spain, the Irish Consulate and a fantastic charity called Prisoners Abroad. We are now more confident that Wayne will be released without charge at some point soon and we will then have the biggest party possible.

On a personal level, I would like to give you, the reader, an everyday example of living with rape. It's now January 2013, the twenty-first to be precise. Several months ago I got reacquainted with friends from my past through Facebook. Just idle chit-chat and the like.

After a while I got sick of explaining to people, individually, that my book was written as a result of being raped. I decided to publicly post on Facebook that my book was indeed about rape and the huge impact this has had on me and those around me.

Many of the old "friends" I had been chatting with stopped chatting to me. I wonder even now, do they not know what to say to me? Or do they think that they won't be able to talk to me? I had to stop myself posting on Facebook, "rape is not catching!"

For the many friends I have made who have been abused and raped as children, I would like to tell you, the reader, another example of my daily life and their lives. I was watching Sky News in my little shop last week when the Savile Report was being discussed, as it had just been released.

The presenter was interviewing a man who had worked for over twenty years with child sex abusers, paedophiles. The presenter was trying to work out why Jimmy Savile was the way he was, and the "expert" said that, in all his time working with these monsters, he had never worked with one who was not abused as a child themselves.

This enraged me and I emailed Sky News. The editor called me almost immediately, and I explained to him that this myth was called the "Vampire Syndrome" and was quite simply a load of shite. I explained to the editor that my many, many male friends, victims of childhood abuse, would never abuse their children, as they knew first-hand the damage that it caused.

I also asked that editor, a nice man, a very thought-provoking question, "Does that mean that I'm going to rape someone, as I have now been raped?"

"Of course not," he said. And he took the "expert" off air.

I have learned through established research that the "vampire syndrome" has developed through our society as abusers often use "their" abuse as an excuse for their inexcusable behaviour.

I am not saying that all abusers have not been abused, as I am sure many have, but as adults we make choices based on our values and beliefs. Whether we have been abused or not does not influence our choice as responsible adults to ruin the life of an innocent child.

On a practical level, as a victim of rape, I have certain restrictions placed on me and my human rights. I asked the courts service in Bolton if I could volunteer for the Victim Support Service and I was told that I could not. I would have to wait at least three years. I am also prohibited from doing jury service, which is something I have always wanted to do. Also, as a result of my PTSD, I may, ironically, not be able to adopt or foster in the future.

I had a call from Duncan recently. He asked if I would be interested in taking part in some research being carried out by the University of East London. The research was trying to understand why most male rape victims don't actually report it. By understanding this, the researchers would hopefully be able to put a case to Government in the hope of increasing services for adult male victims.

I agreed to take part and met a lovely young PhD student, Catherine Pittfield, in Via Fossa. We had a pint and she recorded yet another conversation with me. As I agreed and wanted my name to be used, I am now the co-author of a PhD Thesis. Now Dad would be proud.

Apart from the obvious stigma attached to being any rape victim, I have also had to face the stigma of being in therapy. I struggle to understand why society places these stigmas on people and I am proud to say that I am still in therapy. I enjoy meeting with the lads from Survivors and am proud, really proud, of the real friendships I have made.

I also made some new and really, really good friends when I decided it was time for me to start the process of changing my career and set about looking for a counselling course. I found a level two course and signed up. It was to be delivered at the Inspire Centre on Stockport Road in Levenshulme. Jason, another Survivor and my very good friend, decided to do the course with me and one wet Wednesday morning we started on our journey to the centre.

I wasn't expecting an old converted church, which had been tastefully transformed into a community type centre with lots of interesting activities going on, all community based and led. I parked the car and we walked in, quite nervously, as we had no clue what to expect. We were early, and when we went inside there was a group of people sitting around some tables chatting. A middle-aged lady with a kind face approached us and asked if we were there for the counselling course. This was the first time we met Mrs Joan Manville, our tutor on the course.

After a while we got ourselves settled into a classroom and Joan did something which I had done many times in my social care career, and indeed had facilitated many times myself when delivering training. She asked us to chat with the student next to us and to introduce that person to the rest of the group. Pretty normal training start-up, I thought, but for me this was different. I was there because I wanted to change my career and to repay the world of therapy which, let's face it, had got me to this particular place in my life.

So, what the hell, I thought, and another very public disclosure was about to take place. Louise, my "partner", handled it beautifully and stated that I had been raped, as if I had been involved in a car accident. Wow, I thought at the time, she will make a good counsellor.

The course was six weeks' long with attendance twice a week, Wednesdays and Fridays, and I looked forward to it each time; we all did. Friendships were developing and even a romance. Although not everyone completed it, or even passed it, it would leave an impression on me which would change my view of counselling forever and I thank my classmates, now friends, for that but most importantly I thank Joan. A small, kind, gentle lady with a wealth of life experience, which she was willing to share, most importantly she has the most wicked sense of humour used in the most appropriate ways, which I truly respect.

As I am writing this I'm waiting for Facebook "likes", which will indicate permission from my friends on the course to use their names in my book. It's been ten minutes now and I've had three, so I will now take a liberty and write their names anyway, which can always be changed later if they want. The friends I made on the level two counselling course, and who I hope will remain in my life for a very long time, are Rachael, Donna, Louise, Nancy, VJ, Glynn and Stewart.

The most important lesson I learned is a very simple one: the mantra by which every therapist should adhere to, three very simple words, "Do no harm." I got permission and some great words of encouragement from all the guys on the course and Louise sent me a text message saying my words made her feel "sentimentally lovely".

During that course a strange and very beautiful thing happened. I got home that Friday night after ten pm. I'd gone straight from college after an emotional day anyway, but needed to support Danny and the lads, as I had tried to do ever since the birth of The Survivors Manchester Football Club. I was just settling down when the phone rang. It was Lisa, who I hadn't heard from in ages. She told me that our campaign had worked. The hostel where Brian's evil murderer had lived, had been shut down. That moment I cannot explain.

Then another bombshell, but like the news which I had just received, it consumed me with confusion, pride, delight, and excitement. The bombshell was indeed just that, a bombshell. Bettina's hard work had paid off yet again. A plaque is to be erected in her honour and I had just been invited. Well done, Bettina, well fucking done, is all I could hear my head saying. Lisa knew I was crying. I tried to say goodbye but only managed to mouth the words, "thank you" and hung up.

I completed the course and, while considering whether to go for a night out with my new friends to celebrate our achievement, I realised there was something I had signed up to that I probably shouldn't have, the BUPA 10K Run. It was during another course that Duncan had asked me and the lads if we would like to participate in the run.

A motivational speaker, Martin Robert Hall, had offered to facilitate a ten week course on positive thinking called 'The Psychological Edge' for any of the Survivor lads who might be interested. We met once a week in the Gardens Hotel in Manchester city centre and, I must admit, I got a lot from the course. I think I was expecting an American-style 'High Five' type of affair, but I couldn't have got it more wrong.

Martin had written a book called "Success Is Not An Accident" and the course was basically a synopsis of his book. He taught us ways to think more positively, and to adjust our circle of friends in order to have the best possible frame of mind to achieve what we all wanted to achieve in life, whether that be something small or something extraordinary. At the end of the course we had a small party where we presented Martin with a gift, and we each received our certificates and a copy of Martin's book. I would recommend it to anyone thinking of making a change in their lives, whether that be in their personal or business lives.

Anyway, at this party Duncan said we could all do the run to make some money for Survivors, if we wanted to. Danny joked that he wouldn't get any sponsors so I said that if I got the sponsors, he could run in my name and therefore I'd get all the glory. Everyone thought this was funny but

Duncan suggested it may be considered fraud, so that idea went out of the window. I spontaneously agreed to do the run while secretly thinking I can't run across the bleeding road never mind ten kilometres. It was to cost £39 for Duncan to enter each of us, and any sponsorship money raised above this amount would go to your chosen charity, in our case Survivors.

So that was it, from that meeting I was now committed to the BUPA Manchester 10K run, which was to be held on the twenty-sixth of May starting in Portland Street and ending apparently in Deansgate. Now this didn't really sound too bad if you said it quickly, but a surprise was in store on the day.

On the way home I kept thinking I really needed to do some proper training, but I didn't even possess a pair of trainers. Driving home, I put a cunning plan in place; I would not use the car as often as possible and would walk everywhere. My motivation was that, after the rape, I had no car and had to walk in rain and snow to get to and from the shop from that horrible flat in Newton Heath. If I could do it then, surely I could do a ten kilometre run?

We were having a shit summer so, hopefully, on the day it would be cool and with any luck it may even rain, I thought. Another part of my plan was to use the footie club each Friday night as my training venue, whilst the lads were playing five-a-side at the Pitts in Ardwick Green. I would run around the perimeter of the pitch and, surely, that would be enough training? I couldn't forget that I am forty-three and not seventeen but, hey, I'd give it a go.

Every Friday night at six thirty I'd make my way to the Pitts, sometimes with Jason, and I did actually put my training plan in place. I'd told the lads originally that my role on the footie team was to do some cheerleading and hand out the orange segments at half time, but I was actually enjoying the training. I stuck to my guns when it came to getting the bus rather than using the car and I walked everywhere, usually with the now impressive Jaya, who had grown so big that if he had been white and not wolf grey I would have almost had my beloved Tex back. He is so like him in every way; kind and gentle but clumsy with an unimaginable sense of fun and mischief behind thoughtful and inquisitive eyes. He hadn't yet developed his taste in music, but there was plenty of time for that.

The training continued with long Sunday walks for Jaya, I would try to avoid the city centre unless in a group, as I had always to be aware that the monster was still out there and generally his movements were contained to the centre of the city and in particular the Gay Village. However, I had been in the village with friends many times since his release, but had never seen him. I'd try to forget this and never brought it up in conversation, but this was my reality and I suppose, deep down, I did want to see him, just to see if it would cause an episode of PTSD. I now had this under my own invisible control but it was, and still is, a condition I battle daily.

One Sunday morning at three thirty am I decided to test my PTSD to the highest possible extent. I got ready, wearing black jeans, my new black trainers and a black cotton hoodie. I wore black leather gloves and went to find my knife; it had gradually been moved from under my bed to its rightful place in the silver rack next to the cooker. It was a carving knife with a wooden handle. I put Jaya in the back of the car and we drove with intent, into the Gay Village. It was dead, apart from the odd reveller waiting for a cab or being sick.

I parked the car at the back of Queer Bar and waited until it was really quiet before getting out of the car. I took a strong hold of Jaya's lead and off we went, on the hunt for a rapist. We walked our way slowly around the village and I gradually convinced myself that what I was doing was ridiculous, if not a little dangerous. What would I do if I saw him? Could I use a knife on another human being? Just find him, John, and kill him. Kill him, John, he raped you. Snap out of this shit and get home, this is your father speaking.

That last thought brought me to my, now exhausted, senses and I did just as Dad said and got into the car and drove calmly home. I put the knife back in the silver rack and vowed never to even think about that again. The following day I giggled inside, at least it had been an extra bit of training.

The big day came, the BUPA TEN KILOMETRE RUN. Someone had said there would be around ten thousand runners, all running to support their own charities. Duncan had arranged for us all to meet at the Quaker Hall so, after getting changed into my trackie bottoms and T-shirt, I put on my new trainers. I say new, they were now three months old but looked brand new; not a good sign, I thought.

The next thing to check was the weather; oh my God! It was sweltering out there. The forecast said it would be the hottest day of the summer so far. Fuck! I got my water and man bag and drove into town. The city centre was in lockdown; no cars were allowed in so I had to find a parking space, which could not have been further from the Quaker Hall, Grosvenor Street off Oxford Road.

I parked up and started the gentle walk to the hall. There were lots of other runners, maybe a few hundred or so all getting prepared for the run. By the time I got to the hall I was knackered, what with the heat and burning sun. How the fuck was I going to complete this race? Danny and I had joked on a day out that we would intentionally come last. The thinking was that we would get maximum publicity for Survivors. However, that thinking could now very well become a reality for all the wrong reasons.

Duncan and a few of the lads had arrived early and all looked fine in their Survivors Manchester vests, with their running numbers pinned on the front. Duncan gave me my vest and we chatted about the run. The first surprise was the length of the course. It wasn't starting from Portland Street and ending at Deansgate, as I had thanked God for. It did indeed start at Portland Street and ended at Deansgate, but someone seemed to forget to tell me that it went all the way up Chester Road to the poxy United ground before the mammoth trek back to Deansgate. My God! I thought, the United ground wasn't even in Manchester so I wasn't doing a Manchester run at all, I was doing a cross border run. This couldn't get any better, I thought.

The next surprise was the number of people running; not the vast ten thousand strong crowd, but an incredible forty thousand truly inspirational people who were willing to do this for their chosen charities. I'd seen many thousands of people together at a concert and had been a part of the one million people who had gathered in the Phoenix Park in Dublin to see the Pope when I was ten, but I had never run in a crowd of forty thousand people and I'd imagined that it would be like fleeing from the Taliban in some war-torn country.

I was here now and it was actually happening, so I did some warming up and stretching exercises with the other lads. We were in the green wave which didn't set off till eleven fifty, so we had plenty of time. In my rush in the morning, I'd forgotten to grab my GPS device which was to be inserted into my trainer. This was to monitor my race time and would be used to capture photos of me and the other runners, which would be taken periodically, as we ran or walked, or dragged ourselves around the course. In my case, maybe I wouldn't finish so the GPS device would be academic anyway.

I got myself prepared as best I could and, just as I was psyching myself up for actually doing this, the phone rang. It was Danny. Not Danny, who had done my PTSD picture or the beautiful poem, 'Them Three', but another Survivor who had also become a true friend and whose daughter, Grace, was to end up designing and producing the cover of my book, for which I will be eternally grateful. The original cover had become the subject of a copyright issue which, thank God, I had managed to resolve.

Danny was on his way in to support the Survivors and, although he had originally planned to run himself, he couldn't as his knee injury had not been resolved. Before he got to the hall I mentioned out loud that I had forgotten my GPS tracker thing. I really wasn't bothered that I'd forgotten mine and joked to the lads that I didn't really need to see my finishing time all over the internet, and I certainly didn't want pictures of me looking like a mad woman from Borneo running through the streets of Manchester, or Trafford for that matter.

Then Duncan said, "You need to get a new one, John, it's really important. Anything could happen and we need to know where you are." He may as well have said, "He's still out there", as that is what I heard in my head. But then he was right and, as much as I had tried to resolve this in my own mind, the truth was that the Monster was still out there, unmonitored and allowed to do what he liked, whether he be on the Sex Offenders' Register or not.

When Danny arrived a few minutes later I asked him to walk with me to the Charities Tent in the GMEX, only a short walk away. It was crammed with people – spectators, supporters, volunteers and runners, plus the usual sprinkling of emergency services and St John's Ambulance, which tended to support such events. As we walked up the steps of the GMEX to the entrance, we were chatting about nothing in particular when I remembered a day of which this reminded me. That beautiful warm May day the previous year when Indie, Jaya and I went to receive her Endal award.

I joked with Danny that Jaya had shit all over the red carpet and Lee had been fuming. He had to clean it up whilst continually saying, "Keep those fucking cameras away from me." Danny thought this was hilarious, and at the time it had been, but not for poor Lee.

We went inside the crowded foyer of the charity tent and went over to join the long queue of runners who had some reason to seek assistance. When we eventually got to the counter, the nice young girl with a friendly face and great smile asked me what my name was. I told her and waited for some remark or other, but she casually fiddled with her computer and said, "Imagine", whilst raising her eyebrows in a very slow and condescending manner.

"I've heard that a thousand times, hun," I said rather triumphantly. "What?" she asked, a bit confused. "Imagine, John Lennon," I said, expecting her to understand. She very abruptly said, "Imagine losing your tracker an hour before the run." Now I did feel really stupid but she re-registered my name and gave me a new number and tracker. I thanked her and she wished me and the other Survivors luck.

Danny and I made our way back to the others and we made our final preparations for the run. Duncan was to play cloakroom assistant and wait there until we all gathered at the end of the run. If I make it at all, is what I was thinking, but I was here now, surrounded by other Survivors and friends.

That morning I'd had what seemed like hundreds of calls and texts wishing me luck and telling me they'd watch out for me on BBC2, which was covering the event from start to finish. I'd do the best I could and consoled myself that if I didn't finish, I'd repay all the sponsorship money and make a donation of whatever I could afford to Survivors.

The time came. Me and four other runners from Survivors made our way to Portland Street, where we were to be both entertained and "warmed up" by three people – two men and a woman, who were performing on a small platform raised above us by a crane. There were runners everywhere, thousands and thousands of us all running for charity, but what caught my eye from the start was that the main charity theme was cancer. The Christie, Cancer Research UK, and every other cancer charity. Just as we were finishing our next, and I hoped last, dance/warm-up routine, my phone rang. It was Yvonne. The noise from the crowd was too loud and we were shouting at each other and not speaking.

"Good luck!" she screamed.

"Thanks, hun," I screamed back.

"Do it for our dads."

That made my heart sink but I didn't want to scream a reply, so I said as loudly as I could, whilst trying to remain focused and as unemotional as possible, "I will." My eyes filled with tears that I could not control, despite all my best efforts.

Danny saw this and said, "Are you ok, mate?"

"I'm fine, just the heat you know," I replied, thinking, what has Yvonne done?

Just as I was composing myself, there was a mention of Drummer Lee Rigby. I was expecting a minute's silence or something, but we were all asked to cheer as loud as we could for young Lee and we did. The noise was rapturous, and in my head and heart I'd prayed that his family would not only see it reported on TV but would actually hear this most respectful of noises from their home in Middleton. We cheered as loud as we possibly could, and then the time came and we were off.

Gentle jog at first, as people positioned themselves in between the runners they were with, but after maybe five minutes we got to Deansgate Lock and my efforts as a runner were starting to show their true colours. Danny and Lee, the new Vice Chair of Survivors, stayed with me until I realised that I was holding them back. I was running, or at least jogging – in this heat, for me that was an achievement – but I didn't want to hold them back. So when we got to the lock I said, under hugely laboured breaths, "Go, lads, I'll be fine." Danny asked if I would be ok and I nodded profusely whilst trying to breathe and not cough up my lungs. They got the message and I slowed down or they speeded up, I'm not sure which.

I ran and ran as best I could, trying to ignore the other runners; the promotions of Manchester, of BUPA, the other charities, the runners who needed St John's Ambulance, the crowds, thousands of people who had come to support their friends, their families, their chosen charities and their work places. I was there not for Survivors, I was there for Dad. As I ran, the only thing that kept me going was my dad, my father, the great Plumbob.

I ran in a straight line as best I could and prayed for some shade, but there was none. I joked later that whoever designed the course must have held secret ambitions to be a mass murderer, because they were dropping like flies and St John's Ambulance was stretched to capacity. Many runners looked as though they had severe sunstroke combined with pure exhaustion. Some runners had to stop to vomit and some lay flat out on the road in spread-eagle fashion; they just gave up. However, I knew that whatever money they had raised would actually be given to their charities because, like them, I knew I would do exactly the same if I didn't finish the course.

My running could be described as a gentle jog, fading into a military-style march with swinging arms. I tried not to catch anybody else's attention. I could barely breathe and knew that speaking was definitely out of the question. I ran and ran for what seemed an eternity, but I was doing it, and each time I looked behind me there were thousands of other runners. Some would overtake me in a proud sprint, but I got to overtake them later in the race.

I looked to the beautiful crisp blue sky a few times and said in my head, "How am I doing, Dad?" Maybe it was delirium or maybe it was the start of heatstroke, but I very clearly heard Dad, "Go on, son, you can do it."

I kept repeating this mantra over and over again until the sound from the crowds was silence, pure silence. I could no longer hear any of the other runners' words of encouragement or indeed any of the spectators who were throwing beautiful words of encouragement. All I could hear was Dad's voice, "Go on, son, you can do it." And do it, I did. I crossed the finish line in one hour, twenty one minutes and six seconds.

"I've done it, Dad, I did it for you." These words I repeated until I could actually speak without gasping for

breath and wanting to vomit. When I had recovered enough to walk and breathe normally, I was given a goodie bag which contained a T-shirt, some energy drinks, and – most importantly – my medal. A beautiful, pewter medal on a rainbow flag patterned ribbon. I met Duncan and the lads at the Quaker Hall and Duncan took this picture of me.

To me it represents victory and maybe recovery, recovery from rape. I'm not too sure, as rape is something you learn to live with, you never truly recover, you just learn to live with it. My mantra for you the reader: Rape is rape full stop, whether man, woman or child.

It seems appropriate to end with one last poem. My friend, Ray Groundland, wrote this poem about me, Wayne and Dad. Ray is not a poet by profession but he has captured the spirit of my book in "John, Wayne and Plumbob".

John, Wayne and Plumbob

None of us are ever born into this world
And can predict our lives
As they begin to unfurl
Some of us don't
Have a say in events
That will change our whole lives
And leave indelible dents
But ALL of us have the option to use
All events good and bad
In this life we don't choose
To better our existence
Whilst here on this earth
And to make sure our life
Becomes a legacy of worth
There's a man that I visit
For a wash, cut and blow
A man that is kind to me
A man with a life filled with woe
A man that has suffered more than ANYONE need
A man that when I first visited
I lifted my leg and then peed
I am gifted because
My daddy protects ME
From the bad in this world
The harm I don't see
But this man I do visit

Has suffered more than his fair
share, of life's suffering
His life it would scare
Any regular person
Of a life that is blessed
His character and strength
Has been put to the test.
This man is of a family
A family of love
But who really knows
What HE above
Has in store for each one
of us, as our existence unfolds
This man has suffered
And his story is told
In this book in your hands
In this story you read
This man's life is a story
A trauma indeed.
When not so very young
And in this world well clued,
He was attacked and was raped
And his body abused
By a man not worthy
To walk on this earth
A man consumed with bad
With no value or worth.
That man's now confined
In a prison cell
But there's no recompense for the absolute hell
He created for my friend
His dick should be severed by a large hunting knife
A small price to pay for affecting a life
For the torment won't end
For my friend and my groomer
But his torment doesn't stop there

For there is more even gloomier.
My friend has a brother, Blinkey, a great guy
With three beautiful daughters that light up his sky
But we're all made different
And Blinkey has rage
As you will understand
Whilst reading this page.
A rage of this level, can only have cost
As a result of this rage,
Someone's life was lost.
Blinkey now pays the price
By way of repentance
As he suffers in prison
Whilst serving a sentence
But if this wasn't enough
My friend's torment
Has been only increased by
The loss of a true gent.
My friend's dear father
Has been taken away
By the most horrendous disease
On the planet today
An illness of torture that
No-one should endure
A cruel, terrible illness
That as yet has no cure.
He is now at peace and no longer suffers
But the pain never ends
For the left behind others.
My friend is a good man
With MORE than enough grief
But it's time for my friend
To experience relief
From a terrible life of heartache and pain
Time for his happiness to resume again.
Suffering can only strengthen

Character and soul
It can create great strength
And can change your whole
Outlook on life
Your spirit and élan
It is the greatest catalyst
of life known to man.
My friend is a good man
Who has suffered indeed
But he has converted his suffering
Into sewing a seed
Of hope for all people
In all kinds of pain
That it is never too late
To LIVE again.
they call it a dog's life
But I am just lucky
That my greatest concern
Is when my paws are all mucky.
I like my friend John
And I look forward to when
I need a bath and a trim
And I see my friend again

Maxie Gee, Cavalier King Charles Spaniel.

Ray Groundland: r.groundland@sky.com

Goodbye, My Journey To Justice?